ESSAYS ON CIVIL DISOBEDIENCE

DOVER THRIFT EDITIONS

Edited by
Bob Blaisdell

DOVER PUBLICATIONS
GARDEN CITY, NEW YORK

DOVER THRIFT EDITIONS

GENERAL EDITOR: SUSAN L. RATTINER
EDITOR OF THIS VOLUME: JANET B. KOPITO

ACKNOWLEDGMENTS: See page xi.

Bibliographical Note

Essays on Civil Disobedience, first published by Dover Publications in 2016, is a new compilation of essays, reprinted from standard editions. Bob Blaisdell has selected the essays and provided the introductory Note and brief biographies. Spelling inconsistencies and the like derive from the sources and have been retained for the sake of authenticity.

Library of Congress Cataloging-in-Publication Data

Names: Blaisdell, Robert, editor.
Title: Essays on civil disobedience / edited by Bob Blaisdell.
Description: Garden City, New York : Dover Publications, 2016. |
Series: Dover thrift editions
Identifiers: LCCN 2015039464| ISBN 9780486793818 (paperback) |
  ISBN 0486793818 (paperback)
Subjects: LCSH: Civil disobedience. | BISAC: HISTORY / Americas (North,
  Central, South, West Indies). | HISTORY / Modern / 20th Century. |
  LITERARY COLLECTIONS / Essays.
Classification: LCC JC328.3 .E85 2016 | DDC 303.6/1--dc23
LC record available at http://lccn.loc.gov/2015039464

Manufactured in the United States of America
79381806   2021
www.doverpublications.com

Note

IT'S HARDER TO say what civil disobedience is than what it *does*. What it does is prick our conscience to consider the morality of a particular law. Then it attempts to persuade us that the law being disobeyed is unjust. If civil disobedience results in its participants being arrested or attacked, no violence is returned. In court or in public media, persuasion will be attempted again. Civil disobedience is a brave and necessarily lonely and outnumbered action. The philosopher Tony Milligan has tried to define civil disobedience right up to and including the Occupy Wall Street protests of 2011–2012, and concedes that the idealism of practicing civil disobedience, being a human endeavor, necessarily has failures: "Even if we take a comparatively minimal view of what civil disobedience involves, i.e. non-violent but principled law-breaking, it may be pointed out that from Spain to London, and from San Francisco to Zuccotti Park, there was sporadic violence. Such violence, albeit at a low level, could hardly be avoided given the movement's scale and diversity, not to mention its refusal to sanction any disciplining leadership."[1] The definition of civil disobedience, ever since Henry David Thoreau's fierce expression of it in 1849 popularized its name, changes depending on who's invoking it: "In a sense, there simply is no single agreed-upon concept of civil disobedience that has proven stable over the course of time."[2] Perhaps the best definition that Milligan has found is the one roughed out by the American philosopher John Rawls: "It is 'a public nonviolent,

---

[1] Tony Milligan. *Civil Disobedience: Protest, Justification, and the Law.* New York and London: Bloomsbury. 2013. 9–10.
[2] *Ibid.* 13.

conscientious yet political act contrary to law usually done with the aim of bringing about a change in the law or policies of the government. By acting in this way one addresses the sense of justice of the majority of the community and declares that in one's considered opinion the principles of social co-operation among free and equal men are not being respected.'"[3]

We know that Mahatma Gandhi inspired a vast and important civil disobedience movement in his native India and relied on overcoming religious prejudices and differences. But there is no gainsaying that its origins, as understood by the giant of Russian civil disobedience, Leo Tolstoy, belonged to the principle of nonresistance described by Jesus Christ in the Sermon on the Mount in the Gospel According to Matthew: "Ye have heard that it hath been said, An eye for an eye, and a tooth for a tooth: but I say unto you, That ye resist not evil: but whosoever shall smite thee on thy right cheek, turn to him the other also."[4] Tolstoy believed that the sense of morality was inherent in every person ("The Kingdom of God is Within You") and was independent of dogmatic religion. He insisted that the value of Jesus' principles were founded on their truth rather than on Jesus' status as a divinity. His excited discussions in books and essays of his understanding of Christ's teachings brought him into conflict with the Russian church and state, whose power-sharing had resulted in continual warfare with other nations and peoples, and at home in the subjugation of tens of millions of peasants. Tolstoy proved (to his and our satisfaction) that the violent actions of the "civilized world," the Russian church and government included, contradicted the most fundamental Christian beliefs: "After eighteen hundred years of education in Christianity the civilized world, as represented by its most advanced thinkers, holds the conviction that the Christian religion is a religion of dogmas; that its teaching in relation to life is unreasonable, and is an exaggeration, subversive of the real lawful obligations of morality consistent with the nature of man; and that very doctrine of retribution which Christ rejected, and in place of which he put his teaching, is more practically useful for us.

"To learned men the doctrine of nonresistance to evil by force is exaggerated and even irrational. Christianity is much better without

---

[3] *Ibid.* 14. Milligan is quoting from Rawls's *A Theory of Justice* (Cambridge, Massachusetts, 1971), page 364.

[4] The Holy Bible, King James version. New York: American Bible Society. 1999.

it, they think, not observing closely what Christianity, as represented by them, amounts to.

"They do not see that to say that the doctrine of nonresistance to evil is an exaggeration in Christ's teaching is just like saying that the statement of the equality of the radii of a circle is an exaggeration in the definition of a circle. And those who speak thus are acting precisely like a man who, having no idea of what a circle is, should declare that this requirement, that every point of the circumference should be an equal distance from the center, is exaggerated. To advocate the rejection of Christ's command of nonresistance to evil, or its adaptation to the needs of life, implies a misunderstanding of the teaching of Christ."[5]

The utopian minister Adin Ballou, much less famous than his contemporary civilly disobedient fellow Americans William Lloyd Garrison and Henry David Thoreau, happily answered a favorite criticism of the absolute pacifism he practiced: "I do firmly believe that in acting out these principles steadily and consistently, I shall continue longer uninjured, longer in the enjoyment of life, and longer safe from the depredations, assaults, and murderous violence of wicked men than with all the swords, guns, pistols, dirks, peace officers, sheriffs, judges, prisons, and gallows of the world. If this is the faith of a fool, then am I willing to be accounted a fool, until time shall test the merits of my position. It may not prove to be such great folly after all. 'Well,' says the objector, 'I should like to know how you would manage matters if the ruffian should actually break into your house with settled intent to rob and murder. Would you shrink back like a coward and see your wife and children slaughtered before your eyes?' I cannot tell how I might act in such a dreadful emergency—how weak and frail I should prove. But I can tell how I ought to act—how I should wish to act. If I am a firm, consistent non-resistant, I should prove myself no coward; for it requires the noblest courage and the highest fortitude to be a true non-resistant. If I am what I ought to be, I should be calm and unruffled by the alarm at my door. I should meet my wretched fellow-man with a spirit, an air, a salutation, and a deportment so Christ-like, so little expected, so confounding, and so morally

---

[5] Leo Tolstoy. "Christianity Misunderstood by Men of Science" (Chapter 4), in *The Kingdom of God Is Within You*. Translated by Constance Garnett. Mineola, New York: Dover, 2012.

irresistible that in all probability his weapons of violence and death would fall harmless to his side."[6]

Sixty-five years later Tolstoy was also answering the taunting critics of nonresistance: "The other day in one of the most progressive periodicals I read the opinion of an educated and intelligent writer, expressed with complete assurance in its correctness, that the recognition by me of the principle of nonresistance to evil by violence is a lamentable and somewhat comic delusion which, taking into consideration my old age and certain merits, can only be passed over in indulgent silence.

"Exactly the same attitude towards this question did I encounter in my conversation with the remarkably intelligent and progressive American [William Jennings] Bryan. He also, with the evident intention of gently and courteously showing me my delusion, asked me how I explained my strange principle of nonresistance to evil by violence, and as usual he brought forward the argument, which seems to everyone irrefutable, of the brigand who kills or violates a child. I told him that I recognize nonresistance to evil by violence because, having lived seventy-five years, I have never, except in discussions, encountered that fantastic brigand, who, before my eyes, desired to kill or violate a child, but that perpetually I did and do see not one but millions of brigands using violence towards children and women and men and old people and all the laborers in the name of the recognized right of violence over one's fellows. When I said this my kind interlocutor, with his naturally quick perception, not giving me time to finish, laughed, and recognized that my argument was satisfactory.

"No one has seen the fantastic brigand, but the world, groaning under violence, lies before everyone's eyes. Yet no one sees, nor desires to see, that the strife which can liberate man from violence is not a strife with the fantastic brigand, but with those actual brigands who practise violence over men.

"Nonresistance to evil by violence really means only that the mutual interaction of rational beings upon each other should consist not in violence (which can be only admitted in relation to lower organisms deprived of reason) but in rational persuasion; and that, consequently, towards this substitution of rational persuasion for

---

[6] See page 6.

coercion all those should strive who desire to further the welfare of mankind."[7]

Tolstoy spent much of the last thirty years of his life advocating for civil disobedience, continually putting himself in danger of reprisals from the government and the church. The effectiveness of civil disobedience was so threatening to the unjust social order that Gandhi and Martin Luther King, Jr., were eventually assassinated for, if among other reasons, their adherence to peaceful protest. Our living contemporaries Aung San Suu Kyi and Nadezhda Tolokonnikova have suffered for their commitment to justice and their willingness to participate in civil disobedience. Perhaps Aleksandr Solzhenitsyn's famous admonition is the sharpest and clearest directive: "Live Not by Lies." Following this rule is bound to lead anyone into civil disobedience.

In making these selections, which could have been limited to essays by the four most famous authors on civil disobedience, Thoreau, Tolstoy, Gandhi and King, I have tried to keep the focus on them while offering a few more examples of other brave and admirable practitioners up to our own times. Tony Milligan's *Civil Disobedience: Protest, Justification, and the Law* (2013) is a provocative study; among the best anthologies on our theme is David R. Weber's *Civil Disobedience in America: A Documentary History* (1978). I thank Professor Michael Denner, editor of *Tolstoy Studies Journal*, for sharing his thoughts about Tolstoy's ideas of "nonaction" in *The Kingdom of God is Within You.*

—Bob Blaisdell
New York City,
January 2016

---

[7] "What I Owe to Garrison" by Leo Tolstoi [sic]. In V. Tchertkoff and F. Holah's *A Short Biography of William Lloyd Garrison*. London: The Free Age Press. 1904. 52.

Contents

ACKNOWLEDGMENTS

"The 'Two Percent' Speech," by Albert Einstein, reprinted with permission from The Albert Einstein Archives at The Hebrew University of Jerusalem.

"Civil Disobedience and the Threat of Nuclear Warfare," by Bertrand Russell, Reprinted with Permission from The Bertrand Russell Peace Foundation.

"Love, Law, and Civil Disobedience," Dr. Martin Luther King Jr., copyright © 1961 by Dr. Martin Luther King, Jr., © renewed 1989 by Coretta Scott King; "Letter from Birmingham City Jail" copyright © 1963 by Dr. Martin Luther King, Jr., © renewed 1991 by Coretta Scott King. Reprinted by arrangement with The Heirs to the Estate of Martin Luther King, Jr., c/o Writers House as agent for the proprietor New York, NY.

"Live Not By Lies," by Aleksandr Solzhenitsyn, reprinted with permission from ISI Books.

"Words Will Break Cement," Nadezhda Tolokonnikova, translated by Masha Gessen, from *Words Will Break Cement: The Passion of Pussy Riot* by Masha Gessen, copyright © 2014 by Masha Gessen. Used by permission of Riverhead, an imprint of Penguin Publishing Group, a division of Penguin Random House LLC.

WILLIAM LLOYD GARRISON

The Declaration of Sentiments Adopted by the Peace Convention (1838)

The Liberator, Vol. VIII. No. 39 (September 28, 1838)

Best known for his brave and relentless campaign for the abolition of slavery in the United States, William Lloyd Garrison (1805–1879) also distinguished himself for his commitment to civil disobedience, or, in his terms, "nonresistance." Not only as an author but as a speaker, noted one of his contemporaries, he delivered "a rain of fire."[1] The Peace Convention was a national political group committed to pacifism and based in Boston; "The Declaration of Sentiments Adopted by the Peace Convention" was published in Garrison's abolitionist newspaper, The Liberator, *on September 28, 1838. The Russian novelist and peace activist Leo Tolstoy was inspired by Garrison's life and writings and remarked, "Garrison understood that which the most advanced among the fighters against slavery did not understand: that the only irrefutable argument against slavery is the denial of the right of any man over the liberty of another under any conditions whatsoever." Tolstoy concluded, "Therefore Garrison will forever remain one of the greatest reformers and promoters of true human progress."[2]*

ASSEMBLED IN CONVENTION, from various sections of the American Union, for the promotion of peace on earth and good-will among men, we, the undersigned, regard it as due to ourselves, to the cause which we love, to the country in which we live, and to the world, to publish a *declaration,* expressive of the principles

---

[1] Goldwin Smith. *The Moral Crusader, William Lloyd Garrison: A Biographical Essay.* New York: Funk and Wagnalls. 1892. 97.

[2] "What I Owe to Garrison" by Leo Tolstoi. In V. Tchertkoff and F. Holah's *A Short Biography of William Lloyd Garrison.* London: The Free Age Press. 1904. 49, 55.

we cherish, the purposes we aim to accomplish, and the measures we shall adopt to carry forward the work of peaceful, universal reformation.

We cannot acknowledge allegiance to any human government; neither can we oppose any such government by a resort to physical force. We recognize but one **King** and **Lawgiver**, one **Judge** and **Ruler** of mankind. We are bound by the laws of a kingdom which is not of this world; the subjects of which are forbidden to fight; in which **Mercy** and **Truth** are met together, and **Righteousness** and **Peace** have kissed each other; which has no state lines, no national partitions, no geographical boundaries; in which there is no distinction of rank, or division of caste, or inequality of sex; the officers of which are **Peace**, its extractors **Righteousness**, its walls **Salvation**, and its gates **Praise**; and which is destined to break in pieces and consume all other kingdoms.

Our country is the world, our countrymen are all mankind. We love the land of our nativity only as we love all other lands. The interests, rights, liberties of American citizens are no more dear to us than are those of the whole human race. Hence, we can allow no appeal to patriotism, to revenge any national insult or injury. The **Prince of Peace**, under whose stainless banner we rally, came not to destroy, but to save, even the worst of enemies. He has left us an example, that we should follow his steps. **God commandeth his love toward us, in that while we were yet sinners, Christ died for us**.

We conceive, that if a nation has no right to defend itself against foreign enemies, or to punish its invaders, no individual possesses that right in his own case. The unit cannot be of greater importance than the aggregate. If one man may take life, to obtain or defend his rights, the same license must necessarily be granted to communities, states, and nations. If *he* may use a dagger or a pistol, *they* may employ cannon, bomb-shells, land and naval forces. The means of self-preservation must be in proportion to the magnitude of interests at stake and the number of lives exposed to destruction. But if a rapacious and bloodthirsty soldiery, thronging these shores from abroad, with intent to commit rapine and destroy life, may not be resisted by the people or magistracy, then ought no resistance to be offered to domestic troublers of the public peace or of private security. No obligation can rest upon Americans to regard foreigners as more sacred in their persons than themselves, or to give them a monopoly of wrong-doing with impunity.

The dogma, that all the governments of the world are approvingly ordained of God, and that **the powers that be** in the United States, in Russia, in Turkey, are in accordance with his will, is not less absurd than impious. It makes the impartial Author of human freedom and equality, unequal and tyrannical. It cannot be affirmed that **the powers that be**, in any nation, are actuated by the spirit or guided by the example of Christ, in the treatment of enemies; therefore, they cannot be agreeable to the will of God, and therefore, their overthrow, by a spiritual regeneration of their subjects, is inevitable.

We register our testimony, not only against all wars, whether offensive or defensive, but all prepations for war; against every naval ship, every arsenal, every fortification; against the militia system and a standing army; against all military chieftains and soldiers; against all monuments commemorative of victory over a fallen foe, all trophies won in battle, all celebrations in honor of military or naval exploits; against all appropriations for the defence of a nation by force and arms, on the part of any legislative body; against every edict of government requiring of its subjects military service. Hence, we deem it unlawful to bear arms, or to hold a military office.

As every human government is upheld by physical strength, and its laws are enforced virtually at the point of the bayonet, we cannot hold any office which imposes upon its incumbent the obligation to compel men to do right, on pain of imprisonent or death. We therefore voluntarily exclude ourselves from every legislative and judicial body, and repudiate all human politics, worldly honors, and stations of authority. If *we* cannot occupy a seat in the legislature or on the bench, neither can we elect *others* to act as our substitutes in any such capacity.

It follows, that we cannot sue any man at law, to compel him by force to restore anything which he may have wrongfully taken from us or others; but if he has seized our coat, we shall surrender up our cloak, rather than subject him to punishment.

We believe that the penal code of the old covenant, **An eye for an eye and a tooth for a tooth**, has been abrogated by **Jesus Christ**; and that, under the new covenant, the forgiveness instead of the punishment of enemies has been enjoined upon all his disciples, in all cases whatsoever. To extort money from his enemies, or set them upon a pillory, or cast them into prison, or hang them upon a gallows, is obviously not to forgive, but to take retribution. **Vengeance is mine—I will repay, saith the Lord.**

The history of mankind is crowded with evidence proving that physical coercion is not adapted to moral regeneration; that the sinful disposition of men can be subdued only by love; that evil can be exterminated from earth only by goodness; that it is not safe to rely on an arm of flesh, upon a man whose breath is in his nostrils, to preserve us from harm; that there is great security in being gentle, harmless, long-suffering, and abundant in mercy; that it is only the meek who shall inherit the earth, for the violent who resort to the sword are destined to perish with the sword. Hence, as a measure of sound policy—of safety to property, life, and liberty—of public quietude and private enjoyment—as well as on the ground of allegiance to *Him* who is **King of kings and Lord of lords**, we cordially adopt the non-resistance principle; being confident that it provides for all possible consequences, will ensure all things needful to us, is armed with omnipotent power, and must ultimately triumph over every assailing force.

We advocate no jacobinical doctrine. The spirit of jacobinism is the spirit of retaliation, violence, and murder. It neither fears God nor regards man. *We* would be filled with the spirit of **Christ**. If we abide by our principles, it is impossible for us to be disorderly or plot treason, or participate in any evil work; we shall submit to every ordinance of man, **for the Lord's sake**; obey all the requirements of Government, except such as we deem contrary to the commands of the gospel; and in no case resist the operation of the law, except by meekly submitting to the penalty of disobedience.

But, while we shall adhere to the doctrine of non-resistance and passive submission to enemies, we purpose, in a moral and spiritual sense, to speak and act boldly in the cause of God; to assail iniquity, in high places and in low places; to apply our principles to all existing civil, political, legal, and ecclesiastical institutions; and to hasten the time when the kingdoms of this world will have become the kingdoms of our **Lord** and of his **Christ**, and he shall reign for ever.

It appears to us a self-evident truth, that, whatever the gospel is designed to destroy at any period of the world, being contrary to it, ought now to be abandoned. If, then, the time is predicted when swords shall be beaten into ploughshares, and spears into pruning-hooks, and men shall not learn the art of war any more, it follows that all who manufacture, sell or wield these deadly weapons, do thus array themselves against the peaceful dominion of the Son of God on earth.

Having thus briefly, but frankly, stated our principles and purposes, we proceed to specify the measures we propose to adopt, in carrying our object into effect.

We expect to prevail through **the foolishness of preaching**— striving to commend ourselves unto every man's conscience, in the sight of **God**. From the press, we shall promulgate our sentiments as widely as practicable. We shall endeavour to secure the cooperation of all persons, of whatever name or sect. The triumphant progress of the cause of **Temperance** and **Abolition** in our land, through the instrumentality of benevolent and voluntary associations, encourages us to combine our own means and efforts for the promotion of a still greater cause. Hence, we shall employ lecturers, circulate tracts and publications, form societies, and petition our State and national governments, in relation to the subject of **Universal Peace**. It will be our leading object to devise ways and means for effecting a radical change in the views, feelings, and practices of society, respecting the sinfulness of war and the treatment of enemies.

In entering upon the great work before us, we are not unmindful that, in its prosecution, we may be called to test our sincerity, even as in a fiery ordeal. It may subject us to insult, outrage, suffering, yea, even death itself. We anticipate no small amount of misconception, misrepresentation, calumny. Tumults may arise against us. The ongodly and violent, the pround and pharisaical, the ambitious and tyrannical, principalities and powers, and spiritual wickedness in high places, may combine to crush us. So they treated the **Messiah**, whose example we are humbly striving to imitate. If we suffer with him, we know that we shall reign with him. We shall not be so afraid of their terror, neither be troubled. Our confidence is in the **Lord Almighty**, not in man. Having withdrawn from human protection, what can sustain us but that faith which overcomes the world? We shall not think it strange concerning the fiery trial which is to try us, as though some strange thing had happened unto us; but rejoice, inasmuch as we are partakers of **Christ's** sufferings. Wherefore, we commit the keeping of our souls to God, in well-doing, as unto the faithful Creator. **For every one that forsakes houses, or brethren, or sisters, or father, or mother, or wife, or children, or lands, for Christ's sake, shall receive a hundred fold, and shall inherit everlasting life.**

Firmly relying upon the certain and universal triumph of the sentiments contained in this *declaration*, however formidable may be the opposition arrayed against them—in solemn testimony of our faith in their divine origin—we hereby affix our signatures to it; commending it to the reason and conscience of mankind, giving ourselves no anxiety as to what may befall us, and resolving in the strength of the **Lord God** calmly and meekly to abide the issue.

ADIN BALLOU

Non-Resistance in Relation to Human Governments (1839)

First Annual Meeting, Non-Resistance Society, Boston (September 25, 1839)

Adin Ballou (1803–1890) was a reverend who founded the utopian community at Hopedale in Massachusetts. There is less fierceness in Ballou's passionate writing than in Garrison's; he was equally insistent, however, in declaring his commitment to non-resistance and that its first and vital practitioner was Jesus Christ: "Hence he made himself the great Exemplar of non-resistants; and 'when he was reviled, reviled not again; when he suffered, he threatened not; but committed himself to Him that judgeth righteously'; enduring every insult, reproach, cruelty, and torture of his enemies with unprovokable patience and unconquerable love; forgiving his most deadly persecutors, and expiring with a prayer upon his lips for their salvation. Thus he overcame evil with good and, leaving behind him the Alexanders and Caesars of this world in their base murderous glory, earned for himself a name which is above every name, whether in this world or that to come ..." In advocating the conscientious use of civil disobedience (not so-called by him) Ballou reflects: "The conclusion is therefore unavoidable, that the will of man (human government)—whether in one, a thousand, or many millions—has no intrinsic authority, no moral supremacy, and no rightful claim to the allegiance of man. It has no original, inherent authority whatsoever over the conscience."

Friend President—"WHERE THE SPIRIT of the Lord is, there is liberty." I feel that the Spirit of the Lord is in this meeting, and that all who participate in its discussions are at liberty to express their convictions and peculiar views in their own way, without fear of offending each other. We are of various religious connections, and have not only different opinions on many points, but different modes of thought and expression. Be it so, since we come together in love, for the consideration and promotion of that grand virtue of Christianity without which all others become practically unfruitful.

For my own part, I am not only not offended at hearing opinions and ideas expressed here contrary in some respects to my own, but I am happy to hear them delivered with that freedom and independence which evinces the absence of even a suspicion that anyone can take offence. This is a sure presage of the triumph of truth over all our errors, whatever they may be, or whoever may hold them.

My views of the subject presented in the resolution just submitted may not entirely coincide with those of my friends; but I offer them frankly, expecting that they will be accepted or rejected, as each individual may judge that they deserve.

I perceive with joy that a divine instinct, if so I may term it, actuates my brethren and sisters of this convention in favor of non-resistance. This instinct is as strong and true as the needle to the pole, while at the same time few of us clearly understand how a non-resistant should carry out his principles, especially with respect to human government. The heart is right, though the head may err. "We love the blessed principle of non-resistance, though perhaps we are not sufficiently acute and discriminating, either to state or defend it always correctly. Hence we are not to be argued down by polemic ingenuity and eloquence; which, however confounding, are yet unconvincing that on the whole we are not right. If I can contribute anything towards a better understanding of this important subject, so as to obviate any of its seeming difficulties, I shall deem myself happy in the privilege of being for a few moments a speaker.

The resolution before us is in these words: "Resolved, that it is the object of *this Society* neither to purify nor to subvert human governments, but to advance in the earth that kingdom of peace and righteousness, which supersedes all such governments." In speaking to this resolution, I do so, not formally and technically in the name of this Society (of which I am not a member) but simply as a non-resistant, in defense of the common cause in which we are all engaged. I therefore take the resolution as if it read: "Resolved, that it is the object of *all true non-resistants . . .*" What then are the primary points which it embraces? It seems to suggest three general inquiries: what is human government, what is divine government, and what is the object of non-resistants with respect to human government?

What is human government? It is the will of man—whether of one, a few, many, or all in a state or nation—exercising absolute authority over man, by means of cunning and physical force. This will may be ascertained, declared and executed, with or without written constitutions and laws, regularly or irregularly, in moderation or in violence; still it is alike human government under all forms and administrations, the will of man exercising absolute authority over man, by means of cunning and physical force. It may be patriarchal, hierarchical, monarchical, aristocratic, democratic, or mobocratic— still it answers to this definition. It originates in man, depends on man, and makes man the lord—the slave of man.

What is the divine government? It is the infallible will of God prescribing the duty of moral agents, and claiming their primary undivided allegiance, as indispensable to the enjoyment of pure and endless happiness. In the resolution it is denominated "the kingdom and reign of Christ." The kingdom of Christ is the kingdom of God, for what is Christ's is God's. The Father dwells in the Son, and without Him the Son can do nothing. In this kingdom the all-perfect God is sole King, Lawgiver, and Judge. He divides his authority with no creature; he is absolute Sovereign; he claims the whole heart, mind, and strength. His throne is in the spirit, and he writes his law on the understanding. Whosoever will not obey him implicitly is not yet delivered from the kingdom of darkness, and abides in moral death.

From this it appears that human government, properly so called, can in no case be either superior to, or coequal with, the divine. Can this conclusion be avoided? There are three, and only three cases, in which human government may dispute supremacy with the divine. 1. When God requires one thing and man requires the contrary. In this case, who ought we to obey? All Christians must answer, with the faithful apostles of old, "We ought to obey God rather than men." But must we disobey parents, patriarchs, priests, kings, nobles, presidents, governors, generals, legislatures, constitutions, armies, mobs—all rather than disobey God? We MUST, and then patiently endure the penal consequences. Then surely human government is nothing against the government of God. 2. Human government and divine government sometimes agree in prescribing the same duty; *i.e.* God and man both require the same thing. In this case ought not the reverence of human authority to constitute at least a part of the motive for doing right? We will see. Did man originate this duty? No. Did he first declare it? No. Has he added one iota of obligation to it? No. God originated it, first declared it, and made it in the highest possible degree obligatory. Human government has merely borrowed it, re-echoed it, and interwoven it with the tissue of its own enactments. How then can the Christian turn his back on Jehovah, and make his low obeisance to man? Or how can he divide his reverence between the divine and mere human authority? How can he perform this duty any more willingly or faithfully, because human government has re-enacted it? Evidently he cannot. He will feel that it is the Creator's law, not the creature's; that he is under the highest possible obligation to perform it from reverence to God alone. Man has adopted it, and incorporated it with his own devices, but he has added nothing to its rightfulness or force. Here again human government is virtually nothing. It has not even a claim of joint reverence, with that of the divine. 3. Human legislators enact many laws for the relief, convenience, and general welfare of mankind, which are demonstrably right and salutary, but which God never expressly authorized in detail. In this case has not human authority a primary claim to our reverence? Let us see. What is the motive from which a true Christian will perform these requirements of man? Must he not first be convinced that they are in perfect harmony with the great law of love to God and man— that they agree with what the divine Lawgiver has expressly required? Doubtless. Well, when fully convinced of this, what are they to him but mere amplifications of the heavenly law—new applications of its plain principles—more minute details of acknowledged general duty? What, therefore, is demonstrably right, he will feel bound to approve and scrupulously practice, not for human government's sake, but for righteousness' sake—or, in other words, for the divine government's sake. This must be his great motive, for no other would be a holy motive. It is one thing to discover new items of duty—new applications of moral obligation—and another to create them. Man may discover and point out new details— circumstantial peculiarities of duty—but he cannot create principles, nor originate moral obligation. The infinite Father has preoccupied this whole field. What then if the legislature discovers a new item of duty, arising out of a new combination of circumstances, and enacts a good law for the observance of that duty, with pains and penalties annexed; or what if a convention like this discovers the existence of such an item of duty, and affirms it in the form of a solemn resolution; the duty once made plain, no matter how, would not the truly good man be under precisely the same obligation to perform it? And if the legislature should afterwards without cause repeal such a law, and enact a bad one in its stead; or if this convention should repudiate the existence of the duty before declared, would not the enlightened Christian still be under precisely the same obligation? None of these supposed circumstances ought to weigh a feather upon the conscience. The sense of obligation must look directly to the Great Source of moral perfection, and the grand controlling motive of a holy heart in the performance of every duty must be, *God requires it—it is right—it is best*. We must perform all our duties as unto God, and not unto man.

The conclusion is therefore unavoidable, that the will of man (human government)—whether in one, a thousand, or many millions—has no intrinsic authority, no moral supremacy, and no rightful claim to the allegiance of man. It has no original, inherent authority whatsoever over the conscience. What then becomes of human government, as contradistinguished from the divine government? Is it not a mere cipher? When it opposes God's government, it is nothing; when it agrees with his government, it is nothing; and when it discovers a new item of duty—a new application of the general law of God—it is nothing.

We now arrive at the third inquiry suggested in the resolution before us: what is the object of non-resistants with respect to human government? Is it their object to purify it, to reform it? No, for our principles forbid us to take any part in the management of its machinery. We can neither fight for it, legislate in it, hold its offices, vote at its elections, nor act any political part within its pale. To purify, to reform it—if such were our object—we must actively participate in its management. Moreover, if human government, properly so called, is what I have shown it to be, there can be no such thing as purifying it. Where there is nothing but dross, there is nothing to refine. Separate from what is commonly considered human government all that it has borrowed, or stolen from the divine, and what remains? What is there in the merely human that is worth purifying—capable of purification? Nothing. Again, is it our object to subvert human government—to overthrow it—to turn it upside down? By no means. We utterly disclaim any such object. We are no Jacobins, Revolutionists, or Anarchists—though often slanderously called such. And here I must be permitted to make some explanations, demanded by the public misapprehension of our real position and general movement. It seems to be taken for granted that we have started a crusade to force the practice of non-resistance upon nations, states, bodies politic, and all existing organizations of human society. This is considered tantamount to an attempt for the violent subversion of human government, and is a very great mistake. We are not so insane as to imagine any such result practicable in the nature of things. We put our enterprise on purely Christian grounds, and depend for success wholly on the use of Christian means. We have nothing to do with nations, states, and bodies politic, merely as such, for they have neither souls nor consciences. We address ourselves to individuals, who have both soul and conscience, and expect to affect organized masses of men only through their individual members. And as to any kind of force, other than that of truth and love sustained by a consistent example, as non-resistants, we utterly eschew it, with respect to all moral agents, collectively and individually. We very well know that neither bodies politic, nor individuals, can practice Christian non-resistance while actuated by the spirit of this world and void of Christian principle—that is to say, while they are radically anti-Christian in feeling, motive, conduct, and moral character. We are not so wild and visionary as to expect such impossibilities. Nor do we go against all human government in favor of no government. We make no such issue. On the contrary, we believe it to be among the irrevocable ordinations of God that all who will not be governed by Him shall be governed by one another; shall be tyrannized over by one another; that so long as men will indulge the lust of dominion, they shall be filled with the fruits of slavery; that they who will not be obedient to the law of love shall bow down under the yoke of physical force; that "they who take the sword shall perish with the sword"; and that while so many as twenty ambitious, proud, selfish, revengeful, sinful men remain in any corner of the world, they shall be subject to a human government of physical violence among themselves. If men will make themselves sick, medicine is a necessary evil. If they will not observe the laws of health, they must bow to the dictation of doctors. If they will be gluttons, drunkards, debauchees, and pugilists, they must make the best of emetics, cathartics, cautery, amputation, and whatever else ensues. So if men will not be governed by God, it is their doom to be enslaved one by another. And in this view, human government—defective as it is, bad as it is—is a necessary evil to those who will not be in willing subjection to the divine.[1] Its restraints are better than no restraints at all—and its evils are preventives of greater ones. For thus it is that selfishness is made to

---

[1] These arguments remind the transcriber of the words of Petr Chelčický: "The man who obeys God needs no other authority over him."

thwart selfishness, pride to humble pride, revenge to check revenge, cruelty to deter cruelty, and wrath to punish wrath; that the vile lusts of men, overruled by infinite wisdom, may counteract and destroy each other. In this way human government grows out of the disorder of rebellious moral natures, and will continue, by inevitable consequence, in some form or other among men, until He whose right it is to reign "shall be all in all." In the meantime, non-resistants are required by their principles not to resist any of the ordinances of these governments by physical force, however unjust and wicked; but to be subject to the powers that be, either actively or passively. Actively, in doing whatever they require that is agreeable to the law of God, or which may be innocently consented to. Passively, in patiently suffering their penalties, whenever duty to the divine government requires that man should be disobeyed. No unnecessary offence is to be given to Caesar, but his tribute money is to be rendered to him and his taxes quietly paid, while at the same time the things which belong to God are to be most scrupulously rendered to Him, regardless alike of the favor or the frowns of all the governments on earth.

What then is the object of non-resistants with respect to human governments—if it is neither to purify nor subvert them? The resolution declares that it is to supersede them. To supersede them with what? With the kingdom of Christ. How? By the spiritual regeneration of their individual subjects—by implanting in their minds higher principles of feeling and action—by giving them heavenly instead of earthly motives. And now, to understand this process of superseding, let us consider the nature of Christ's kingdom. It is not an outward, temporal kingdom, like those of this world. It is spiritual, moral, and eternal. When the Jews demanded information about the coming of this kingdom, ignorantly expecting it to appear with unparalleled external majesty, pomp, and circumstance, Jesus replied, "The kingdom of God cometh not with observation. Neither shall men say, 'lo here,' or 'lo there,' for behold, the kingdom of God is within you." When before Pilate, charged by his enemies with having set himself up against Caesar as a king, he said, "My kingdom is not of this world. If my kingdom were of this world, then my servants would fight, that I should not be delivered to the Jews. But now is my kingdom not from hence." When his yet worldly-minded disciples strove among themselves which should be greatest in his kingdom, he washed their feet with his own hands for an example, and declared to them that he among them who would be greatest should be least of all, and servant of all. He forbade them to exercise lordship after the manner of carnal men among the nations of the earth, but to esteem each other better than themselves, and to regard humility as the only true greatness and to vie with each other—not for the highest, but for the lowest place—not for a chance to rule, but for a chance to serve—not for the blessedness of receiving, but for that of giving—not for the praise of man, but for the approval of God—not for the prerogative of inflicting physical suffering for righteousness' sake, but for the privilege of enduring it. Hence he made himself the great Exemplar of non-resistants; and "when he was reviled, reviled not again; when he suffered, he threatened not; but committed himself to Him that judgeth righteously"; enduring every insult, reproach, cruelty, and torture of his enemies with unprovokable patience and unconquerable love; forgiving his most deadly persecutors, and expiring with a prayer upon his lips for their salvation. Thus he overcame evil with good and, leaving behind him the Alexanders and Caesars of this world in their base murderous glory, earned for himself a name which is above every name, whether in this world or that to come; being highly exalted at the divine right hand, "that unto him every knee should bow, of things in heaven, in earth, and under the earth—and every tongue confess him Lord to the glory of God the Father." Such is the Lord and Master of Christians, whom they are to obey and imitate, rather than Moses, or Samuel, or David, or Solomon, or Elijah, or Daniel, or even John. His kingdom is the kingdom of heaven, wherein all legislative, judicial, and avenging power is vested exclusively in that High and Holy One, who cannot err, either in sentiment, judgment, or action. Of this kingdom the apostle truly says that it "is not meat and drink, but righteousness, and peace, and joy in the Holy Ghost." The fruit of its spirit, he further says, "is love, joy, peace, long-suffering, gentleness, goodness, faith, meekness, and temperance." "Now they that are Christ's have crucified the flesh with its affections and lusts." Having learned to renounce carnal weapons of defense, worldly honors, political preferences, and a vain dependence on the operations of human government for the cure of moral disorders, they cease to avenge themselves on evil-doers, either on their own responsibility as individuals, or on that of the state through its penal laws. They deem it their duty to forgive, not punish—to yield unto wrath and suffer wrong, without recompensing evil for evil—referring their cause always unto Him who has said, "Vengeance is mine; I will repay,"—and thus obeying Christ in his injunction to love enemies, bless them that curse, do good to them that hate, and pray for the despiteful and persecuting.

This is the doctrine and practice which non-resistants profess to have embraced, and according to the tenor of which they propose to supersede all human government with the divine. This is the real object of their present movement. They cease to take any active part in the affairs of human government. They cease to put their trust in the wisdom of man for guidance, or in the arm of flesh for protection. Yet they stand not in the attitude of antagonists to human government; nor can they allow themselves to be mistaken for anarchists and be considered as willing to give any just cause of offence to the "powers that be." Neither can they enter into any quarrel with professedly good men, who feel called to no higher mission than that of reigning or serving in the kingdoms of this world. But we hear a voice from above, saying, "What is that to thee? Follow thou me." And we deem it our privilege, through whatever of reproach or suffering we may be called, to show unto all good men whose reliance is even secondarily upon human government for the conversion of the world, "a more excellent way." And now, what is there so horrible, so dangerous, so alarming in all this? Why are we so misunderstood, misrepresented, and denounced? These principles and this cause must prevail—if Christianity itself shall prevail—and blessed are they among our opposers, whose mistaken zeal shall not betray them into warfare against God.

But the cry salutes our ears from the open mouths even of professing Christians, "Non-resistance is impracticable in the present state of the world; you must wait until the millennium." I answer, "To him that believeth, all things are possible." Let the power of love and forbearance be faithfully exemplified, and it will remove mountains. And as to the millennium, what is it? Is it a state of things to come about like the seasons, by the revolution of the planets? Is it to be the result of some arbitrary mechanical process, or of a mere chemical agency? Is it to be the effect of physical or of moral causes? Alas! How many are expecting the millennium to come "with observation," just as the Jews of old were expecting the kingdom of God, not knowing that this millennium and kingdom must be within men before it can ever be around them. Let us have the spirit of the millennium, and do the works of the millennium. Then will the millennium have already come, and then will it speedily embosom the whole earth. What is this cry of impracticability, but a cry of rebellion against the living God? Although under preliminary dispensations he winked at the ignorance of mankind, and even commanded his chosen servants to act a conspicuous part in the great system of governmental violence, this was only until "the times of reformation." In Christ He annuls the temporary ordinances of revenge and commands forbearance—non-resistance to the physical violence of man, even of the most injurious. Hear his *Revised Statutes:* "Ye have heard that it hath been said, 'An eye for an eye, and a tooth for a tooth': but I say unto you, that ye resist not evil; but whosoever shall smite thee on thy right cheek, turn to him the other also. And if any man will sue thee at the law, and take away thy coat, let him have thy cloak also." Now is it impracticable to obey this holy commandment? Is not God the best judge of what is practicable? Who has a right to question the expediency or practicability of what the Infinite Father through his Son has enjoined. And let us be careful not to narrow down the meaning of this commandment. It is much more comprehensive than most expositors have been willing to allow. It forbids not merely all personal, individual, self-assumed right of retaliation, but all revenge at law—all procuring of punishment to our injurers in the way of legal prosecution and judicial sentence. It goes this whole length. When our Lord says, "Ye have heard that it hath been said, 'An eye for an eye and a tooth for a tooth,'" he refers to the Mosaic Law. By consulting Exodus 21: 22–25, Leviticus 24: 19–20, and Deuteronomy 19: 18–21, we find the Law referred to, according to which it must be given "life for life, breach for breach, eye for eye, tooth for tooth, hand for hand, foot for foot, burning for burning, wound for wound, and stripe for stripe." The injured party, or his friends in his stead, had their redress and revenge at law. They might not take the business into their own hands, but had to enter their complaint in due form to the elders of their town or city, and have a fair trial of the accused before the proper tribunals. When the sentence of the judges had been pronounced, it was executed in legal form; the criminal being doomed to suffer the same injury to life or limb that he had caused to his neighbor. Thus when a man had received a wound from his fellow man, or lost an eye, or a tooth, a hand or a foot, he had his revenge at law, by due process of which he could thrust out an eye, or a tooth, or cut off a hand or a foot, or inflict any other injury that had been inflicted on him. But however salutary this statute, and however necessary to the good order of society in the opinion of political moralists, the great Master of Christians has abrogated it, and commanded his followers not to resist evil; not to resist it even according to law—not to procure punishment to their injurers through the regular judicial medium, but to bear all indignities, insults, assaults and wrongs with forgiving meekness and patience. Here then is an end to controversy with all who mean to be wholly Christ's: they must be non-resistants. Who dares to question the rectitude, propriety, practicability, or expediency of doing what the all-wise God has thus plainly required? Is it one who calls Christ Lord and Master? Alas for the faithless, distrustful man! Do not such men hear the words of Christ, in just reproof saying, "Why do ye call me Lord, Lord, and do not do the things which I command?"

But all this passes for nothing with many, who exclaim, "What are you going to do with the wolves and tigers of human kind? Are you going to give them full range for their prey? Will you invite the thief, the robber, the burglar, or the murderer to come and carry off your property, ravish away your treasures, spoil your house, butcher your wife and children, and shed your own heart's blood? Will you be such a fool, such an enemy to yourself, your family, and society? Will you encourage all manner of rapine and bloodshed by assurances that you will never resist, nor even prosecute the basest ruffians? What a terrible appeal is this, so full of frightful images and horrid anticipations of evil from the practice of non-resistance? But if I am a Christian, will such appeals move me? Am I a Christian, and do I doubt that God will protect me and mine against all the thieves, robbers, and murderers in the world while I conscientiously do my duty? Am I more willing to rely upon forbidden means of defense than upon the power of Him who does his will in the armies of heaven and among the inhabitants of the earth, and who has said, "I will never leave thee, nor forsake thee"? "But are you sure that God will always render your property, person, and life secure from these attacks?" No, for it may be best that I should suffer—that I should even lose all things earthly. What then, is treasure on earth my only treasure? Is worldly substance my chief good? Is this life my only life? What if I should actually lose my money—have I not treasure laid up in heaven, where neither moth, nor rust, nor thieves can touch it? What if I should suffer great cruelties in my person "for righteousness sake"—should I therefore be miserable? What if I should lose my own life and that of my family—should I not find life eternal for them and myself? I may be robbed, but I shall still be rich; I may be murdered, but I shall live forevermore; I may suffer the loss of all things earthly, but I shall gain all things heavenly. If I cannot confidently say this, am I a Christian? "Who then shall harm us, if we are followers of that which is good?" I have a right to expect, and I do confidently expect, that in practicing the sublime virtue of non-resistance for the kingdom of heaven's sake, God will keep all that I commit to him in perfect safety, even here on earth, as long as it is for my good to be exempted from loss and suffering. I do firmly believe that in acting out these principles steadily and consistently, I shall continue longer uninjured, longer in the enjoyment of life, and longer safe from the depredations, assaults, and murderous violence of wicked men than with all the swords, guns, pistols, dirks, peace officers, sheriffs, judges, prisons, and gallows of the world. If this is the faith of a fool, then am I willing to be accounted a fool, until time shall test the merits of my position. It may not prove to be such great folly after all. "Well," says the objector, "I should like to know how you would manage matters if the ruffian should actually break into your house with settled intent to rob and murder. Would you shrink back like a coward and see your wife and children slaughtered before your eyes?" I cannot tell how I might act in such a dreadful emergency—how weak and frail I should prove. But I can tell how I ought to act—how I should wish to act. If I am a firm, consistent non-resistant, I should prove myself no coward; for it requires the noblest courage and the highest fortitude to be a true non-resistant. If I am what I ought to be, I should be calm and unruffled by the alarm at my door. I should meet my wretched fellow-man with a spirit, an air, a salutation, and a deportment so Christ-like, so little expected, so confounding, and so morally irresistible that in all probability his weapons of violence and death would fall harmless to his side. I would say, "Friend, why do you come here? Surely not to injure those who wish you nothing but good? This house is one of peace and friendship to all mankind. If you are cold, warm yourself at our fire; if hungry, refresh yourself at our table; if you are weary, sleep in our bed; if you are destitute, poor, and needy, freely take of our goods. Come, let us be friends, that God may keep us all from evil and bless us with his protection." What would be the effect of such treatment as this? Would it not completely overcome the feelings of the invader, so as either to make him retreat inoffensively out of the house, or at least forbear all meditated violence? Would it not be incomparably safer than to rush to the shattered door, half distracted with alarm, grasping some deadly weapon and bearing it aloft, looking fiery wrath and mad defiance at the enemy? How soon would follow the mortal encounter, and how extremely uncertain the outcome? The moment I appeared in such an attitude (just the thing expected), would not ruffian's coolness and well-trained muscular force be almost sure to seal the fate of my family and myself? But in acting the non-resistant part, should I not be likely, in nine cases out of ten, to escape with perfect safety? ("Yes," said a brother, "in ninety-nine cases out of a hundred.") Yes, and perhaps nine hundred and ninety-nine out of a thousand. Not however, to expect too much; suppose the robber should not be wholly deterred; would he, at worst, seek anything beyond mere booty? Would not our lives and persons escape untouched? It would hardly be worth his while to murder or mangle those who opposed no force to his depredations. But we will make the case utterly desperate. Contrary to all probability, we will suppose that no moral majesty, no calm and dignified remonstrance, and no divine interposition availed anything towards the prevention of the slaughter of an innocent family; what then would I do in the last resort? I would gather my loved ones in a group behind my person; I would cover their retreat to the farthest corner of our room; and there in their front would I receive the blows of the murderer. I would say to him, "Since nothing but our blood will satisfy your thirst, I commend my all to that God in whom I trust. He will receive us to his bosom, and may He have mercy on you. Strike if you will, but you must come through my poor body to the bodies of these helpless victims!" Well, suppose the horrible tragedy is complete and our butchered remains are all lying silent in their gore; what then? We are all dead; we fell clinging to each other; in a moment the pains of death were over; the "debt of nature" is paid; where are we now? Where? Annihilated? Miserable? No! Our happy spirits, conveyed by holy angels, wing their lightning flight to the bowers of Paradise—to the home of the blest—to the blissful arms of an approving Redeemer—to the welcome embrace "of the just made perfect." Who would not rather pass away thus unstained with blood, into the joys of that Lord, who himself quenched the fiery darts of his malicious murderers with his own vital blood, than to purchase a few days of mortal life by precipitating into eternity a fellow creature, with his millstone of unrepentant crime about his neck? Is it so dreadful a thing for the Christian to be hurried to heaven—to be sent into eternal life a little before his natural time—to have all his pains of dissolution crowded into a moment? Is life on earth, (brief at longest, and often embittered by distressing ills) of so much value, that we would murder, rather than be murdered? Oh, let me die the death of the Christian non-resistant, and let my last end be like His! Let me suffer and die with Christ, that I also may live and reign with him. The conclusion then is, that in a vast majority of cases the non-resistant would remain unharmed by the sons of violence, and that in the worst supposable case, he would only be hurried out of this life, with his dear family, into a better one. But rejoins the objector, "I consider it the duty of a Christian to look to the good of society at large, and to contribute what he can, in a lawful way, to the security of life, person, and property around him. Therefore, let him assist in bringing malefactors to justice, and not shrink from aiding the magistrate in preserving the bulwarks of order." And so we are to throw away God's judgment of what is best, and trample under foot the solemn injunction of Christ! Well, what shall we gain by this infidelity and rebellion? "No, but we are in duty bound to love our neighbor—to seek the peace and welfare of society—to do our part towards protecting the innocent and helpless against the ravages of merciless wolves—to maintain wholesome penal restraints." Answer. We think we are seeking this great end more effectually, as non-resistants, than we could do by becoming informers, prosecutors, jailers, or hangmen. "An ounce of preventive is worth more than a pound of curative." But at all events, since we cannot fight, nor go to law for our dearest relatives or ourselves, we must decline doing so for any other description of persons. It is a favorite argument of our opposers, that we are not required to love our neighbors better than ourselves. Whether this argument is sound or not, perhaps it is not now necessary to affirm; but it is certainly a very conclusive one, or ought to be, with the objector in this case, to show the unreasonableness of requiring us to do more for our neighbors in society at large, than for ourselves, our wives and children. We must act on the same principles and pursue the same general course with respect to all, and in so doing "we stand or fall to our own master."

"But we want the best men in office, the best laws, and the best administration of government. Will you be recreant to your trust as citizens? Will you withhold your votes from the side and cause of right? Will you leave knaves and villains to govern the world?" Answer. We expect to do as much towards keeping the world in order by a straightforward, consistent, exemplary practice of our principles, even more than by voting, office-holding, legislating, or punishing criminals. A truly good man wields an influence on our ground great and salutary wherever he is known. It is not by the poor test of numbers that righteousness can gain its deserved respect in the world. It is not by getting into places of worldly power and emolument that Christians are to promote human welfare. It is not by fighting with carnal weapons, and wielding the instruments of legal vengeance, that they can hope to strengthen the bonds of moral restraint. Majorities often decree folly and iniquity. Power more often corrupts its possessor, than benefits the powerless. The real power that restrains the world is moral power, acting silently and unostentatiously within and upon the soul. He, therefore, who has the fewest outward ensigns of authority, will, if wise and holy, contribute most to the good order of mankind. Besides, even unprincipled men in office are compelled to bow to a strong public sentiment, superinduced by the efforts of good men in private life. They are not wanting in vanity to be esteemed the friends of virtue, and from this motive generally conform their laws and proceedings more or less to a right general opinion. If we can do any thing towards promoting a sound morality, as we hope to do, we shall make our influence felt without envy, not only in the lowest depths of society, but in the high places of political power. I expect, if true to my sense of duty, to do as much in my town and community towards preserving wholesome moral order, as if clothed with the official dignity of a fast select-man,[2] a representative to general court, a justice of the peace, or even a member of Congress. Whatever my natural ambition might have coveted in the blindness of unchastened nature, I now envy not governors, presidents, or monarchs, or their stations of usefulness and glory; but feel that in humble obscurity I have a higher mission assigned me, in the faithful fulfillment of which it may be my privilege to do more for my race, than if elevated to any of their world-envied seats. Every true non-resistant will be a great conservator of public, as well as private morals. Away then with the intrigues and tricks of political ambition, the petty squabbles of partisans and officeholders, the hollow bluster of demagogues, and the capricious admiration of a tickled multitude. Let us obey God, declare the truth, walk in love, and

[2] One of a board of town officers chosen annually in New England communities to manage local affairs.

deserve the gratitude of the world, though we never receive it. "But should non-resistants ever become the great majority in any community, pray how would they get on with public affairs? There must be highways, and bridges, and school houses, and education, and alms-houses, and hospitals." Very well—nothing is easier than for communities of Christian non-resistants to get along with all these matters. Suppose them to meet, in those days, from time to time within each town, or more general community, voluntarily, just as we are here assembled. Suppose them all anxious to know their duty, and ready to do it, as soon as it is clearly pointed out. Then of course the wisest will speak to attentive ears and upright minds. They will propose measures, discuss them in friendship, and come to a conclusion in favor of the best—without wounding personal vanity or breeding a quarrel with each other's selfishness. The law of love and the counsels of wisdom will prevail without strife, and all will be eager to contribute their full share of expense and effort to the object. Instead of the leading few striving, as now, who shall be first and greatest, the strife will then be, who shall have the least authority. And among the mass, instead of the strife, as now, who shall bear the lightest burden, the only strife will be—who shall do most for the promotion of every good work. Happy days, whenever they arrive! If there shall be any poor in those days, or any insane, or any uneducated, or unaccommodated travellers, they will soon be abundantly provided for, without the aid of physical force, pains, or penalties. God hasten that blessed era of love and peace, and grant success to all our well-directed efforts in this holy cause. Thus finally may all human governments be superseded by the divine government, and the kingdoms of this world be swallowed up in the one all-glorious kingdom of our Lord Jesus Christ. And now, having freely expressed my views and feelings on the subject of the resolution presented, I submit them to the consideration of the friends; hoping that they will receive into good and honest hearts whatever is worth retaining, and that the worthless they will cast away.

HENRY DAVID THOREAU

Civil Disobedience (1849)

The author of Walden *and America's foremost writer on man's relation to nature, Henry David Thoreau (1817–1862) was also a forceful lecturer. "Civil Disobedience," the essay in which he made famous the term "civil disobedience," was originally a lecture entitled "Resistance to Civil Government." In it, Thoreau challenges the right of the state, in this case Massachusetts, to override his conscientious objection to the trumped-up Mexican War of 1846–1848 and the abhorrent legalized persistence of slavery. Knowing those governmental undertakings were wrong, he announced that he had no obligation to pay taxes towards their continuance. He presents himself not as a saint but as a sinner himself; he knows, however, that he has access to his own conscience and that the state does not: "I do not hesitate to say, that those who call themselves abolitionists should at once effectually withdraw their support, both in person and property, from the government of Massachusetts, and not wait till they constitute a majority of one, before they suffer the right to prevail through them. I think that it is enough if they have God on their side, without waiting for that other one. Moreover, any man more right than his neighbors, constitutes a majority of one already."*

Though the most famous of all "Civil Disobedience" writings in world literature, it is surprisingly discursive. Some feel that Thoreau is actually at his best when he wanders, where his argument dissipates as his attention fastens on his perceptions of the physical world, in this case his prison cell: "It was like travelling into a far country, such as I had never expected to behold, to lie there for one night. It seemed to me that I never had heard the town-clock strike before, nor the evening sounds of the village; for we slept with the windows open, which were inside the grating. It was to see my native village in the light of the middle ages, and our Concord was turned into a Rhine stream …"

I HEARTILY ACCEPT the motto,—"That government is best which governs least;" and I should like to see it acted up to more rapidly and systematically. Carried out, it finally amounts to this, which also I believe,—"That government is best which governs not at all;" and when men are prepared for it, that will be the kind of government which they will have. Government is at best but an expedient; but most governments are usually, and all governments are sometimes, inexpedient. The objections which have been brought against a standing army, and they are many and weighty, and deserve to prevail, may also at last be brought against a standing government. The standing army is only an arm of the standing government. The government itself, which is only the mode which the people have chosen to execute their will, is equally liable to be abused and perverted before the people can act through it. Witness the present Mexican war, the work of comparatively a few individuals using the standing government as their tool; for, in the outset, the people would not have consented to this measure.

This American government,—what is it but a tradition, though a recent one, endeavoring to transmit itself unimpaired to posterity, but each instant losing some of its integrity? It has not the vitality and force of a single living man; for a single man can bend it to his will. It is a sort of wooden gun to the people themselves; and, if ever they should use it in earnest as a real one against each other, it will surely split. But it is not the less necessary for this; for the people must have some complicated machinery or other, and hear its din, to satisfy that idea of government which they have. Governments show thus how successfully men can be imposed on, even impose on themselves, for their own advantage. It is excellent, we must all allow; yet this government never of itself furthered any enterprise, but by the alacrity with which it got out of its way. *It* does not keep the country free. *It* does not settle the West. *It* does not educate. The character inherent in the American people has done all that has been accomplished; and it would have done somewhat more, if the government had not sometimes got in its way. For government is an expedient by which men would fain succeed in letting one another alone; and, as has been said, when it is most expedient, the governed are most let alone by it. Trade and commerce, if they were not made of India rubber, would never manage to bounce over the obstacles which legislators are continually putting in their way; and, if one were to judge these men wholly by the effects of their actions, and not partly by their intentions, they would deserve to be classed and punished with those mischievous persons who put obstructions on the railroads.

But, to speak practically and as a citizen, unlike those who call themselves no-government men, I ask for, not at once no government, but *at once* a better government. Let every man make known what kind of government would command his respect, and that will be one step toward obtaining it.

After all, the practical reason why, when the power is once in the hands of the people, a majority are permitted, and for a long period continue, to rule, is not because they are most likely to be in the right, nor because this seems fairest to the minority, but because they are physically the strongest. But a government in which the majority rule in all cases cannot be based on justice, even as far as men understand it. Can there not be a government in which majorities do not virtually decide right and wrong, but conscience?—in which majorities decide only those questions to which the rule of expediency is applicable? Must the citizen ever for a moment, or in the least degree, resign his conscience to the legislator? Why has every man a conscience, then? I think that we should be men first, and subjects afterward. It is not desirable to cultivate a respect for the law, so much as for the right. The only obligation which I have a right to assume, is to do at any time what I think right. It is truly enough said, that a corporation has no conscience; but a corporation of conscientious men is a corporation *with* a conscience. Law never made men a whit more just; and, by means of their respect for it, even the well-disposed are daily made the agents of injustice. A common and natural result of an undue respect for law is, that you may see a file of soldiers, colonel, captain, corporal, privates, powder-monkeys and all, marching in admirable order over hill and dale to the wars, against their wills, aye, against their common sense and consciences, which makes it very steep marching indeed, and produces a palpitation of the heart. They have no doubt that it is a damnable business in which they are concerned; they are all peaceably inclined. Now, what are they? Men at all? or small moveable forts and magazines, at the service of some unscrupulous man in power? Visit the Navy Yard, and behold a marine, such a man as an American government can make, or such as it can make a man with its black arts, a mere shadow and reminiscence of humanity, a man laid out alive and standing, and already, as one may say, buried under arms with funeral accompaniments, though it may be

> "Not a drum was heard, nor a funeral note,
>   As his corse to the ramparts we hurried;
> Not a soldier discharged his farewell shot
>   O'er the grave where our hero we buried."

The mass of men serve the State thus, not as men mainly, but as machines, with their bodies. They are the standing army, and the militia, jailers, constables, *posse comitatus,* &c. In most cases there is no free exercise whatever of the judgment or of the moral sense; but they put themselves on a level with wood and earth and stones; and wooden men can perhaps be manufactured that will serve the purpose as well. Such command no more respect than men of straw, or a lump of dirt. They have the same sort of worth only as horses and dogs. Yet such as these even are commonly esteemed good citizens. Others, as most legislators, politicians, lawyers, ministers, and office-holders, serve the State chiefly with their heads; and, as they rarely make any moral distinctions, they are as likely to serve the devil, without intending it, as God. A very few, as heroes, patriots, martyrs, reformers in the great sense, and *men,* serve the State with their consciences also, and so necessarily resist it for the most part; and they are commonly treated by it as enemies. A wise man will only be useful as a man, and will not submit to be "clay," and "stop a hole to keep the wind away," but leave that office to his dust at least:—

> "I am too high-born to be propertied,
> To be a secondary at control,
> Or useful serving-man and instrument
> To any sovereign state throughout the world."

He who gives himself entirely to his fellow-men appears to them useless and selfish; but he who gives himself partially to them is pronounced a benefactor and philanthropist.

How does it become a man to behave toward this American government to-day? I answer that he cannot without disgrace be associated with it. I cannot for an instant recognize that political organization as *my* government which is the *slave's* government also.

All men recognize the right of revolution; that is, the right to refuse allegiance to and to resist the government, when its tyranny or its inefficiency are great and unendurable. But almost all say that such is not the case now. But such was the case, they think, in the Revolution of '75. If one were to tell me that this was a bad government because it taxed certain foreign commodities brought to its ports, it is most probable that I should not make an ado about it, for I can do without them: all machines have their friction; and possibly this does enough good to counterbalance the evil. At any rate, it is a great evil to make a stir about it. But when the friction comes to have its machine, and oppression and robbery are organized, I say, let us not have such a machine any longer. In other words, when a sixth of the population of a nation which has undertaken to be the refuge of liberty are slaves, and a whole country is unjustly overrun and conquered by a foreign army, and subjected to military law, I think that it is not too soon for honest men to rebel and revolutionize. What makes this duty the more urgent is the fact, that the country so overrun is not our own, but ours is the invading army.

Paley, a common authority with many on moral questions, in his chapter on the "Duty of Submission to Civil Government," resolves all civil obligation into expediency; and he proceeds to say, "that so long as the interest of the whole society requires it, that is, so long as the established government cannot be resisted or changed without public inconveniency, it is the will of God that the established government be obeyed, and no longer."—"This principle being admitted, the justice of every particular case of resistance is reduced to a computation of the quantity of the danger and grievance on the one side, and of the probability and expense of redressing it on the other." Of this, he says, every man shall judge for himself. But Paley appears never to have contemplated those cases to which the rule of expediency does not apply, in which a people, as well as an individual, must do justice, cost what it may. If I have unjustly wrested a plank from a drowning man, I must restore it to him though I drown myself. This, according to Paley, would be inconvenient. But he that would save his life, in such a case, shall lose it. This people must cease to hold slaves, and to make war on Mexico, though it cost them their existence as a people.

In their practice, nations agree with Paley; but does any one think that Massachusetts does exactly what is right at the present crisis?

> "A drab of state, a cloth-o'-silver slut,
> To have her train borne up, and her soul trail in the dirt."

Practically speaking, the opponents to a reform in Massachusetts are not a hundred thousand politicians at the South, but a hundred thousand merchants and farmers here, who are more interested in commerce and agriculture than they are in humanity, and are not prepared to do justice to the slave and to Mexico, *cost what it may*. I quarrel not with far-off foes, but with those who, near at home, co-operate with, and do the bidding of those far away, and without whom the latter would be harmless. We are accustomed to say, that the mass of men are unprepared; but improvement is slow, because the few are not materially wiser or better than the many. It is not so important that many should be as good as you, as that there be some absolute goodness somewhere; for that will leaven the whole lump. There are thousands who are *in opinion* opposed to slavery and to the war, who yet in effect do nothing to put an end to them; who, esteeming themselves children of Washington and Franklin, sit down with their hands in their pockets, and say that they know not what to do, and do nothing; who even postpone the question of freedom to the question of free-trade, and quietly read the prices-current along with the latest advices from Mexico, after dinner, and, it may be, fall asleep over them both. What is the price-current of an honest man and patriot today? They hesitate, and they regret, and sometimes they petition; but they do nothing in earnest and with effect. They will wait, well disposed, for others to remedy the evil, that they may no longer have it to regret. At most, they give only a cheap vote, and a feeble countenance and Godspeed, to the right, as it goes by them. There are nine hundred and ninety-nine patrons of virtue to one virtuous man; but it is easier to deal with the real possessor of a thing than with the temporary guardian of it.

All voting is a sort of gaming, like chequers or backgammon, with a slight moral tinge to it, a playing with right and wrong, with moral questions; and betting naturally accompanies it. The character of the voters is not staked. I cast my vote, perchance, as I think right; but I am not vitally concerned that that right should prevail. I am willing to leave it to the majority. Its obligation, therefore, never exceeds that of expediency. Even voting *for the right* is *doing* nothing for it. It is only expressing to men feebly your desire that it should prevail. A wise man will not leave the right to the mercy of chance, nor wish it to prevail through the power of the majority. There is but little virtue in the action of masses of men. When the majority shall at length vote for the abolition of slavery, it will be because they are indifferent to slavery, or because there is but little slavery left to be abolished by their vote. *They* will then be the only slaves. Only *his* vote can hasten the abolition of slavery who asserts his own freedom by his vote.

I hear of a convention to be held at Baltimore, or elsewhere, for the selection of a candidate for the Presidency, made up chiefly of editors, and men who are politicians by profession; but I think, what is it to any independent, intelligent, and respectable man what decision they may come to, shall we not have the advantage of his wisdom and honesty, nevertheless? Can we not count upon some independent votes? Are there not many individuals in the country who do not attend conventions? But no: I find that the respectable man, so called, has immediately drifted from his position, and despairs of his country, when his country has more reason to despair of him. He forthwith adopts one of the candidates thus selected as the only *available* one, thus proving that he is himself *available* for any purposes of the demagogue. His vote is of no more worth than that of any unprincipled foreigner or hireling native, who may have been bought. Oh for a man who is a *man,* and, as my neighbor says, has a bone in his back which you cannot pass your hand through! Our statistics are at fault: the population has been returned too large. How many *men* are there to a square thousand miles in this country? Hardly one. Does not America offer any inducement for men to settle here? The American has dwindled into an Odd Fellow,—one who may be known by the development of his organ of gregariousness, and a manifest lack of intellect and cheerful self-reliance; whose first and chief concern, on coming into the world, is to see that the alms-houses are in good repair; and, before yet he has lawfully donned the virile garb, to collect a fund for the support of the widows and orphans that may be; who, in short, ventures to live only by the aid of the mutual insurance company, which has promised to bury him decently.

It is not a man's duty, as a matter of course, to devote himself to the eradication of any, even the most enormous wrong; he may still properly have other concerns to engage him; but it is his duty, at least, to wash his hands of it, and, if he gives it no thought longer, not to give it practically his support. If I devote myself to other pursuits and contemplations, I must first see, at least, that I do not pursue them sitting upon another man's shoulders. I must get off him first, that he may pursue his contemplations too. See what gross inconsistency is tolerated. I have heard some of my townsmen say, "I should like to have them order me out to help put down an insurrection of the slaves, or to march to Mexico,—see if I would go;" and yet these very men have each, directly by their allegiance, and so indirectly, at least, by their money, furnished a substitute.

The soldier is applauded who refuses to serve in an unjust war by those who do not refuse to sustain the unjust government which makes the war; is applauded by those whose own act and authority he disregards and sets at nought; as if the State were penitent to that degree that it hired one to scourge it while it sinned, but not to that degree that it left off sinning for a moment. Thus, under the name of order and civil government, we are all made at last to pay homage to and support our own meanness. After the first blush of sin, comes its indifference; and from immoral it becomes, as it were, *un*moral, and not quite unnecessary to that life which we have made.

The broadest and most prevalent error requires the most disinterested virtue to sustain it. The slight reproach to which the virtue of patriotism is commonly liable, the noble are most likely to incur. Those who, while they disapprove of the character and measures of a government, yield to it their allegiance and support, are undoubtedly its most conscientious supporters, and so frequently the most serious obstacles to reform. Some are petitioning the State to dissolve the Union, to disregard the requisitions of the President. Why do they not dissolve it themselves,—the union between themselves and the State,—and refuse to pay their quota into its treasury? Do not they stand in the same relation to the State, that the State does to the Union? And have not the same reasons prevented the State from resisting the Union, which have prevented them from resisting the State?

How can a man be satisfied to entertain an opinion merely, and enjoy *it*? Is there any enjoyment in it, if his opinion is that he is aggrieved? If you are cheated out of a single dollar by your neighbor, you do not rest satisfied with knowing that you are cheated, or with saying that you are cheated, or even with petitioning him to pay you your due; but you take effectual steps at once to obtain the full amount, and see that you are never cheated again. Action from principle,—the perception and the performance of right,— changes things and relations; it is essentially revolutionary, and does not consist wholly with any thing which was. It not only divides states and churches, it divides families; aye, it divides the *individual,* separating the diabolical in him from the divine.

Unjust laws exist: shall we be content to obey them, or shall we endeavor to amend them, and obey them until we have succeeded, or shall we transgress them at once? Men generally, under such a government as this, think that they ought to wait until they have persuaded the majority to alter them. They think that, if they should resist, the remedy would be worse than the evil. But it is the fault of the government itself that the remedy *is* worse than the evil. *It* makes it worse. Why is it not more apt to anticipate and provide for reform? Why does it not cherish its wise minority? Why does it cry and resist before it is hurt? Why does it not encourage its citizens to be on the alert to point out its faults, and *do* better than it would have them? Why does it always crucify Christ, and excommunicate Copernicus and Luther, and pronounce Washington and Franklin rebels?

One would think, that a deliberate and practical denial of its authority was the only offence never contemplated by government; else, why has it not assigned its definite, its suitable and proportionate penalty? If a man who has no property refuses but once to earn nine shillings for the State, he is put in prison for a period unlimited by any law that I know, and determined only by the discretion of those who placed him there; but if he should steal ninety times nine shillings from the State, he is soon permitted to go at large again.

If the injustice is part of the necessary friction of the machine of government, let it go, let it go: perchance it will wear smooth,—certainly the machine will wear out. If the injustice has a spring, or a pulley, or a rope, or a crank, exclusively for itself, then perhaps you may consider whether the remedy will not be worse than the evil; but if it is of such a nature that it requires you to be the agent of injustice to another, then, I say, break the law. Let your life be a counter friction to stop the machine. What I have to do is to see, at any rate, that I do not lend myself to the wrong which I condemn.

As for adopting the ways which the State has provided for remedying the evil, I know not of such ways. They take too much time, and a man's life will be gone. I have other affairs to attend to. I came into this world, not chiefly to make this a good place to live in, but to live in it, be it good or bad. A man has not every thing to do, but something; and because he cannot do *every thing,* it is not necessary that he should do *something* wrong. It is not my business to be petitioning the governor or the legislature any more than it is theirs to petition me; and, if they should not hear my petition, what should I do then? But in this case the State has provided no way: its very Constitution is the evil. This may seem to be harsh and stubborn and unconciliatory; but it is to treat with the utmost kindness and consideration the only spirit that can appreciate or deserves it. So is all change for the better, like birth and death which convulse the body.

I do not hesitate to say, that those who call themselves abolitionists should at once effectually withdraw their support, both in person and property, from the government of Massachusetts, and not wait till they constitute a majority of one, before they suffer the right to prevail through them. I think that it is enough if they have God on their side, without waiting for that other one. Moreover, any man more right than his neighbors, constitutes a majority of one already.

I meet this American government, or its representative the State government, directly, and face to face, once a year, no more, in the person of its tax-gatherer; this is the only mode in which a man situated as I am necessarily meets it; and it then says distinctly, Recognize me; and the simplest, the most effectual, and, in the present posture of affairs, the indispensablest mode of treating with it on this head, of expressing your little satisfaction with and love for it, is to deny it then. My civil neighbor, the tax-gatherer, is the very man I have to deal with,—for it is, after all, with men and not with parchment that I quarrel,—and he has voluntarily chosen to be an agent of the government. How shall he ever know well what he is and does as an officer of the government, or as a man, until he is obliged to consider whether he shall treat me, his neighbor, for whom he has respect, as a neighbor and well-disposed man, or as a maniac and disturber of the peace, and see if he can get over this obstruction to his neighborliness without a ruder and more impetuous thought or speech corresponding with his action? I know this well, that if one thousand, if one hundred, if ten men whom I could name,—if ten *honest* men only,—aye, if *one* HONEST man, in this State of Massachusetts, *ceasing to hold slaves,* were actually to withdraw from this copartnership, and be locked up in the county jail therefor, it would be the abolition of slavery in America. For it matters not how small the beginning may seem to be: what is once well done is done for ever. But we love better to talk about it: that we say is our mission. Reform keeps many scores of newspapers in its service, but not one man. If my esteemed neighbor, the State's ambassador, who will devote his days to the settlement of the question of human rights in the Council Chamber, instead of being threatened with the prisons of Carolina, were to sit down the prisoner of Massachusetts, that State which is so anxious to foist the sin of slavery upon her sister,—though at present she can discover only an act of inhospitality to be the ground of a quarrel with her,—the Legislature would not wholly waive the subject the following winter.

Under a government which imprisons any unjustly, the true place for a just man is also a prison. The proper place to-day, the only place which Massachusetts has provided for her freer and less desponding spirits, is in her prisons, to be put out and locked out of the State by her own act, as they have already put themselves out by their principles. It is there that the fugitive slave, and the Mexican prisoner on parole, and the Indian come to plead the wrongs of his race, should find them; on that separate, but more free and honorable ground, where the State places those who are not *with* her but *against* her,—the only house in a slave-state in which a free man can abide with honor. If any think that their influence would be lost there, and their voices no longer afflict the ear of the State, that they would not be as an enemy within its walls, they do not know by how much truth is stronger than error, nor how much more eloquently and effectively he can combat injustice who has experienced a little in his own person. Cast your whole vote, not a strip of paper merely, but your whole influence. A minority is powerless while it conforms to the majority; it is not even a minority then; but it is irresistible when it clogs by its whole weight. If the alternative is to keep all just men in prison, or give up war and slavery, the State will not hesitate which to choose. If a thousand men were not to pay their tax-bills this year, that would not be a violent and bloody measure, as it would be to pay them, and enable the State to commit violence and shed innocent blood. This is, in fact, the definition of a peaceable revolution, if any such is possible. If the tax-gatherer, or any other public officer, asks me, as one has done, "But what shall I do?" my answer is, "If you really wish to do any thing, resign your office." When the subject has refused allegiance, and the officer has resigned his office, then the revolution is accomplished. But even suppose blood should flow. Is there not a sort of blood shed when the conscience is wounded? Through this wound a man's real manhood and immortality flow out, and he bleeds to an everlasting death. I see this blood flowing now.

I have contemplated the imprisonment of the offender, rather than the seizure of his goods,—though both will serve the same purpose,—because they who assert the purest right, and consequently are most dangerous to a corrupt State, commonly have not spent much time in accumulating property. To such the State renders comparatively small service, and a slight tax is wont to appear exorbitant, particularly if they are obliged to earn it by special labor with their hands. If there were one who lived wholly without the use of money, the State itself would hesitate to demand it of him. But the rich man—not to make any invidious comparison—is always sold to the institution which makes him rich. Absolutely speaking, the more money, the less virtue; for money comes between a man and his objects, and obtains them for him; and it was certainly no great virtue to obtain it. It puts to rest many questions which he would otherwise be taxed to answer; while the only new question which it puts is the hard but superfluous one, how to spend it. Thus his moral ground is taken from under his feet. The opportunities of living are diminished in proportion as what are called the "means" are increased. The best thing a man can do for his culture when he is rich is to endeavour to carry out those schemes which he entertained when he was poor. Christ answered the Herodians according to their condition. "Show me the tribute-money," said he;—and one took a penny out of his pocket;—If you use money which has the image of Caesar on it, and which he has made current and valuable, that is, *if you are men of the State,* and gladly enjoy the advantages of Caesar's government, then pay him back some of his own when he demands it; "Render therefore to Caesar that which is Caesar's, and to God those things which are God's,"—leaving them no wiser than before as to which was which; for they did not wish to know.

When I converse with the freest of my neighbors, I perceive that, whatever they may say about the magnitude and seriousness of the question, and their regard for the public tranquillity, the long and the short of the matter is, that they cannot spare the protection of the existing government, and they dread the consequences of disobedience to it to their property and families. For my own part, I should not like to think that I ever rely on the protection of the State. But, if I deny the authority of the State when it presents its tax-bill, it will soon take and waste all my property, and so harass me and my children without end. This is hard. This makes it impossible for a man to live honestly and at the same time comfortably in outward respects. It will not be worth the while to accumulate property; that would be sure to go again. You must hire or squat somewhere, and raise but a small crop, and eat that soon. You must live within yourself, and depend upon yourself, always tucked up and ready for a start, and not have many affairs. A man may grow rich in Turkey even, if he will be in all respects a good subject of the Turkish government. Confucius said,—"If a State is governed by the principles of reason, poverty and misery are subjects of shame; if a State is not governed by the principles of reason, riches and honors are the subjects of shame." No: until I want the protection of Massachusetts to be extended to me in some distant southern port, where my liberty is endangered, or until I am bent solely on building up an estate at home by peaceful enterprise, I can afford to refuse allegiance to Massachusetts, and her right to my property and life. It costs me less in every sense to incur the penalty of disobedience to the State, than it would to obey. I should feel as if I were worth less in that case.

Some years ago, the State met me in behalf of the church, and commanded me to pay a certain sum toward the support of a clergyman whose preaching my father attended, but never I myself. "Pay it," it said, "or be locked up in the jail." I declined to pay. But, unfortunately, another man saw fit to pay it. I did not see why the schoolmaster should be taxed to support the priest, and not the priest the schoolmaster; for I was not the State's schoolmaster, but I supported myself by voluntary subscription. I did not see why the lyceum should not present its tax-bill, and have the State to back its demand, as well as the church. However, at the request of the selectmen, I condescended to make some such statement as this in writing:—"Know all men by these presents, that I, Henry Thoreau, do not wish to be regarded as a member of any incorporated society which I have not joined." This I gave to the town-clerk; and he has it. The State, having thus learned that I did not wish to be regarded as a member of that church, has never made a like demand on me since; though it said that it must adhere to its original presumption that time. If I had known how to name them, I should then have signed off in detail from all the societies which I never signed on to; but I did not know where to find a complete list.

I have paid no poll-tax for six years. I was put into a jail once on this account, for one night; and, as I stood considering the walls of solid stone, two or three feet thick, the door of wood and iron, a foot thick, and the iron grating which strained the light, I could not help being struck with the foolishness of that institution which treated me as if I were mere flesh and blood and bones, to be locked up. I wondered that it should have concluded at length that this was the best use it could put me to, and had never thought to avail itself of my services in some way. I saw that, if there was a wall of stone between me and my townsmen, there was a still more difficult one to climb or break through, before they could get to be as free as I was. I did not for a moment feel confined, and the walls seemed a great waste of stone and mortar. I felt as if I alone of all my townsmen had paid my tax. They plainly did not know how to treat me, but behaved like persons who are underbred. In every threat and in every compliment there was a blunder; for they thought that my chief desire was to stand the other side of that stone wall. I could not but smile to see how industriously they locked the door on my meditations, which followed them out again without let or hinderance, and *they* were really all that was dangerous. As they could not reach me, they had resolved to punish my body; just as boys, if they cannot come at some person against whom they have a spite, will abuse his dog. I saw that the State was half-witted, that it was timid as a lone woman with her silver spoons, and that it did not know its friends from its foes, and I lost all my remaining respect for it, and pitied it.

Thus the State never intentionally confronts a man's sense, intellectual or moral, but only his body, his senses. It is not armed with superior wit or honesty, but with superior physical strength. I was not born to be forced. I will breathe after my own fashion. Let us see who is the strongest. What force has a multitude? They only can force me who obey a higher law than I. They force me to become like themselves. I do not hear of *men* being *forced* to live this way or that by masses of men. What sort of life were that to live? When I meet a government which says to me, "Your money or your life," why should I be in haste to give it my money? It may be in a great strait, and not know what to do: I cannot help that. It must help itself; do as I do. It is not worth the while to snivel about it. I am not responsible for the successful working of the machinery of society. I am not the son of the engineer. I perceive that, when an acorn and a chestnut fall side by side, the one does not remain inert to make way for the other, but both obey their own laws, and spring and grow and flourish as best they can, till one, perchance, overshadows and destroys the other. If a plant cannot live according to its nature, it dies; and so a man.

The night in prison was novel and interesting enough. The prisoners in their shirt-sleeves were enjoying a chat and the evening air in the door-way, when I entered. But the jailer said, "Come, boys, it is time to lock up;" and so they dispersed, and I heard the sound of their steps returning into the hollow apartments. My room-mate was introduced to me by the jailer, as "a first-rate fellow and a clever man." When the door was locked, he showed me where to hang my hat, and how he managed matters there. The rooms were whitewashed once a month; and this one, at least, was the whitest, most simply furnished, and probably the neatest apartment in the town. He naturally wanted to know where I came from, and what brought me there; and, when I had told him, I asked him in my turn how he came there, presuming him to be an honest man, of course; and, as the world goes, I believe he was. "Why," said he, "they accuse me of burning a barn; but I never did it." As near as I could discover, he had probably gone to bed in a barn when drunk, and smoked his pipe there; and so a barn was burnt. He had the reputation of being a clever man, had been there some three months waiting for his trial to come on, and would have to wait as much longer; but he was quite domesticated and contented, since he got his board for nothing, and thought that he was well treated.

He occupied one window, and I the other; and I saw, that, if one stayed there long, his principal business would be to look out the window. I had soon read all the tracts that were left there, and examined where former prisoners had broken out, and where a grate had been sawed off, and heard the history of the various occupants of that room; for I found that even here there was a history and a gossip which never circulated beyond the walls of the jail. Probably this is the only house in the town where verses are composed, which are afterward printed in a circular form, but not published. I was shown quite a long list of verses which were composed by some young men who had been detected in an attempt to escape, who avenged themselves by singing them.

I pumped my fellow-prisoner as dry as I could, for fear I should never see him again; but at length he showed me which was my bed, and left me to blow out the lamp.

It was like travelling into a far country, such as I had never expected to behold, to lie there for one night. It seemed to me that I never had heard the town-clock strike before, nor the evening sounds of the village; for we slept with the windows open, which were inside the grating. It was to see my native village in the light of the middle ages, and our Concord was turned into a Rhine stream, and visions of knights and castles passed before me. They were the voices of old burghers that I heard in the streets. I was an involuntary spectator and auditor of whatever was done and said in the kitchen of the adjacent village-inn,—a wholly new and rare experience to me. It was a closer view of my native town. I was fairly inside of it. I never had seen its institutions before. This is one of its peculiar institutions; for it is a shire town. I began to comprehend what its inhabitants were about.

In the morning, our breakfasts were put through the hole in the door, in small oblong-square tin pans, made to fit, and holding a pint of chocolate, with brown bread, and an iron spoon. When they called for the vessels again, I was green enough to return what bread I had left; but my comrade seized it, and said that I should lay that up for lunch or dinner. Soon after, he was let out to work at haying in a neighboring field, whither he went every day, and would not be back till noon; so he bade me good-day, saying that he doubted if he should see me again.

When I came out of prison,—for some one interfered, and paid the tax,—I did not perceive that great changes had taken place on the common, such as he observed who went in a youth, and emerged a tottering and gray-headed man; and yet a change had to my eyes come over the scene,—the town, and State, and country,—greater than any that mere time could effect. I saw yet more distinctly the State in which I lived. I saw to what extent the people among whom I lived could be trusted as good neighbors and friends; that their friendship was for summer weather only; that they did not greatly purpose to do right; that they were a distinct race from me by their prejudices and superstitions, as the Chinamen and Malays are; that, in their sacrifices to humanity, they ran no risks, not even to their property; that, after all, they were not so noble but they treated the thief as he had treated them, and hoped, by a certain outward observance and a few prayers, and by walking in a particular straight though useless path from time to time, to save their souls. This may be to judge my neighbors harshly; for I believe that most of them are not aware that they have such an institution as the jail in their village.

It was formerly the custom in our village, when a poor debtor came out of jail, for his acquaintances to salute him, looking through their fingers, which were crossed to represent the grating of a jail window, "How do ye do?" My neighbors did not thus salute me, but first looked at me, and then at one another, as if I had returned from a long journey. I was put into jail as I was going to the shoemaker's to get a shoe which was mended. When I was let out the next morning, I proceeded to finish my errand, and, having put on my mended shoe, joined a huckleberry party, who were impatient to put themselves under my conduct; and in half an hour,—for the horse was soon tackled,—was in the midst of a huckleberry field, on one of our highest hills, two miles off; and then the State was nowhere to be seen.

This is the whole history of "My Prisons."

I have never declined paying the highway tax, because I am as desirous of being a good neighbor as I am of being a bad subject; and, as for supporting schools, I am doing my part to educate my fellow-countrymen now. It is for no particular item in the tax-bill that I refuse to pay it. I simply wish to refuse allegiance to the State, to withdraw and stand aloof from it effectually. I do not care to trace the course of my dollar, if I could, till it buys a man, or a musket to shoot one with,—the dollar is innocent,—but I am concerned to trace the effects of my allegiance. In fact, I quietly declare war with the State, after my fashion, though I will still make what use and get what advantage of her I can, as is usual in such cases.

If others pay the tax which is demanded of me, from a sympathy with the State, they do but what they have already done in their own case, or rather they abet injustice to a greater extent than the State requires. If they pay the tax from a mistaken interest in the individual taxed, to save his property or prevent his going to jail, it is because they have not considered wisely how far they let their private feelings interfere with the public good.

This, then, is my position at present. But one cannot be too much on his guard in such a case, lest his action be biassed by obstinacy, or an undue regard for the opinions of men. Let him see that he does only what belongs to himself and to the hour.

I think sometimes, Why, this people mean well; they are only ignorant; they would do better if they knew how: why give your neighbors this pain to treat you as they are not inclined to? But I think, again, this is no reason why I should do as they do, or permit others to suffer much greater pain of a different kind. Again, I sometimes say to myself, When many millions of men, without heat, without ill-will, without personal feeling of any kind, demand of you a few shillings only, without the possibility, such is their constitution, of retracting or altering their present demand, and without the possibility, on your side, of appeal to any other millions, why expose yourself to this overwhelming brute force? You do not resist cold and hunger, the winds and the waves, thus obstinately; you quietly submit to a thousand similar necessities. You do not put your head into the fire. But just in proportion as I regard this as not wholly a brute force, but partly a human force, and consider that I have relations to those millions as to so many millions of men, and not of mere brute or inanimate things, I see that appeal is possible, first and instantaneously, from them to the Maker of them, and, secondly, from them to themselves. But, if I put my head deliberately into the fire, there is no appeal to fire or to the Maker of fire, and I have only myself to blame. If I could convince myself that I have any right to be satisfied with men as they are, and to treat them accordingly, and not according, in some respects, to my requisitions and expectations of what they and I ought to be, then, like a good Mussulman and fatalist, I should endeavor to be satisfied with things as they are, and say it is the will of God. And, above all, there is this difference between resisting this and a purely brute or natural force, that I can resist this with some effect; but I cannot expect, like Orpheus, to change the nature of the rocks and trees and beasts.

I do not wish to quarrel with any man or nation. I do not wish to split hairs, to make fine distinctions, or set myself up as better than my neighbors. I seek rather, I may say, even an excuse for conforming to the laws of the land. I am but too ready to conform to them. Indeed I have reason to suspect myself on this head; and each year, as the tax-gatherer comes round, I find myself disposed to review the acts and position of the general and state governments, and the spirit of the people, to discover a pretext for conformity. I believe that the State will soon be able to take all my work of this sort out of my hands, and then I shall be no better a patriot than my fellow-countrymen. Seen from a lower point of view, the Constitution, with all its faults, is very good; the law and the courts are very respectable; even this State and this American government are, in many respects, very admirable and rare things, to be thankful for, such as a great many have described them; but seen from a point of view a little higher, they are what I have described them; seen from a higher still, and the highest, who shall say what they are, or that they are worth looking at or thinking of at all?

However, the government does not concern me much, and I shall bestow the fewest possible thoughts on it. It is not many moments that I live under a government, even in this world. If a man is thought-free, fancy-free, imagination-free, that which *is not* never for a long time appearing *to be* to him, unwise rulers or reformers cannot fatally interrupt him.

I know that most men think differently from myself; but those whose lives are by profession devoted to the study of these or kindred subjects, content me as little as any. Statesmen and legislators, standing so completely within the institution, never distinctly and nakedly behold it. They speak of moving society, but have no resting-place without it. They may be men of a certain experience and discrimination, and have no doubt invented ingenious and even useful systems, for which we sincerely thank them; but all their wit and usefulness lie within certain not very wide limits. They are wont to forget that the world is not governed by policy and expediency. Webster never goes behind government, and so cannot speak with authority about it. His words are wisdom to those legislators who contemplate no essential reform in the existing government; but for thinkers, and those who legislate for all time, he never once glances at the subject. I know of those whose serene and wise speculations on this theme would soon reveal the limits of his mind's range and hospitality. Yet, compared with the cheap professions of most reformers, and the still cheaper wisdom and eloquence of politicians in general, his are almost the only sensible and valuable words, and we thank Heaven for him. Comparatively, he is always strong, original, and, above all, practical. Still his quality is not wisdom, but prudence. The lawyer's truth is not Truth, but consistency, or a consistent expediency. Truth is always in harmony with herself, and is not concerned chiefly to reveal the justice that may consist with wrong-doing. He well deserves to be called, as he has been called, the Defender of the Constitution. There are really no blows to be given by him but defensive ones. He is not a leader, but a follower. His leaders are the men of '87. "'I have never made an effort," he says, "and never propose to make an effort; I have never countenanced an effort, and never mean to countenance an effort, to disturb the arrangement as originally made, by which the various States came into the Union." Still thinking of the sanction which the Constitution gives to slavery, he says, "Because it was a part of the original compact,— let it stand." Notwithstanding his special acuteness and ability, he is unable to take a fact out of its merely political relations, and behold it as it lies absolutely to be disposed of by the intellect,—what, for instance, it behoves a man to do here in America to-day with regard to slavery, but ventures, or is driven, to make some such desperate answer as the following, while professing to speak absolutely, and as a private man,— from which what new and singular code of social duties might be inferred?—"The manner," says he, "in which the government of those States where slavery exists are to regulate it, is for their own consideration, under their responsibility to their constituents, to the general laws of priority, humanity, and justice, and to God. Associations formed elsewhere, springing from a feeling of humanity, or any other cause, have nothing whatever to do with it. They have never received any encouragement from me, and they never will."*

They who know of no purer sources of truth, who have traced up its stream no higher, stand, and wisely stand, by the Bible and the Constitution, and drink at it there with reverence and humility; but they who behold where it comes trickling into this lake or that pool, gird up their loins once more, and continue their pilgrimage toward its fountain-head.

No man with a genius for legislation has appeared in America. They are rare in the history of the world. There are orators, politicians, and eloquent men, by the thousand; but the speaker has not yet opened his mouth to speak, who is capable of settling the much-vexed questions of the day. We love eloquence for its own sake, and not for any truth which it may utter, or any heroism it may inspire. Our legislators have not yet learned the comparative value of free-trade and of freedom, of union, and of rectitude, to a nation. They have no genius or talent for comparatively humble questions of taxation and finance, commerce and manufactures and agriculture. If we were left solely to the wordy wit of legislators in Congress for our guidance, uncorrected by the seasonable experience and the effectual complaints of the people, America would not long retain her rank among the nations. For eighteen hundred years, though perchance I have no right to say it, the New Testament has been written; yet where is the legislator who has wisdom and practical talent enough to avail himself of the light which it sheds on the science of legislation?

The authority of government, even such as I am willing to submit to,—for I will cheerfully obey those who know and can do better than I, and in many things even those who neither know nor can do so well,—is still an impure one: to be strictly just, it must have the sanction and consent of the governed. It can have no pure right over my person and property but what I concede to it. The

---

* These extracts have been inserted since the Lecture was read. [Thoreau's note.]

progress from an absolute to a limited monarchy, from a limited
monarchy to a democracy, is a progress toward a true respect for
the individual. Is a democracy, such as we know it, the last
improvement possible in government? Is it not possible to take a
step further towards recognizing and organizing the rights of man?
There will never be a really free and enlightened State, until the
State comes to recognize the individual as a higher and independent
power, from which all its own power and authority are derived,
and treats him accordingly. I please myself with imagining a State
at last which can afford to be just to all men, and to treat the individual with respect as a neighbor; which even would not think it
inconsistent with its own repose, if a few were to live aloof from it,
not meddling with it, nor embraced by it, who fulfilled all the
duties of neighbors and fellow-men. A State which bore this kind
of fruit, and suffered it to drop off as fast as it ripened, would prepare the way for a still more perfect and glorious State, which also
I have imagined, but not yet anywhere seen.

HENRY DAVID THOREAU

Slavery in Massachusetts (1854)

An Address, Delivered at the Anti-Slavery Celebration at
Framingham, July 4th, 1854

In "Slavery in Massachusetts," Thoreau questions government in ways that
Tea Partiers today will find familiar and sympathetic, and while his disgust
with the government and majority rule is loud and clear, his primary focus is
individual conscience and human justice. He will not participate, as far as he
is conscious, in the perpetuation of injustice. As in "Civil Disobedience," he
makes the case—in a lecture to his Fourth of July audience at Framingham,
Massachusetts—that the individual must represent himself before ceding his
responsibility: "I would remind my countrymen, that they are to be men first,
and Americans only at a late and convenient hour. No matter how valuable
law may be to protect your property, even to keep soul and body together, if
it do not keep you and humanity together."

I LATELY ATTENDED a meeting of the citizens of Concord, expecting, as one among many, to speak on the subject of slavery in Massachusetts; but I was surprised and disappointed to find that what had called my townsmen together was the destiny of Nebraska, and not of Massachusetts, and that what I had to say would be entirely out of order. I had thought that the house was on fire, and not the prairie; but though several of the citizens of Massachusetts are now in prison for attempting to rescue a slave from her own clutches, not one of the speakers at that meeting expressed regret for it, not one even referred to it. It was only the disposition of some wild lands a thousand miles off, which appeared to concern them. The inhabitants of Concord are not prepared to stand by one of their own bridges, but talk only of taking up a position on the highlands beyond the Yellowstone river. Our Buttricks, and Davises, and Hosmers are retreating thither, and I fear that they will have no Lexington Common between them and the enemy. There is not one slave in Nebraska; there are perhaps a million slaves in Massachusetts.

They who have been bred in the school of politics fail now and always to face the facts. Their measures are half measures and make-shifts, merely. They put off the day of settlement indefinitely, and meanwhile, the debt accumulates. Though the Fugitive Slave Law had not been the subject of discussion on that occasion, it was at length faintly resolved by my townsmen, at an adjourned meeting, as I learn, that the compromise compact of 1820 having been repudiated by one of the parties, 'Therefore, . . . the Fugitive Slave Law must be repealed.' But this is not the reason why an iniquitous law should be repealed. The fact which the politician faces is merely, that there is less honor among thieves than was supposed, and not the fact that they are thieves.

As I had no opportunity to express my thoughts at that meeting, will you allow me to do so here?

Again it happens that the Boston Court House is full of armed men, holding prisoner and trying a MAN, to find out if he is not really a SLAVE. Does any one think that justice or God awaits Mr. Loring's decision? For him to sit there deciding still, when this question is already decided from eternity to eternity, and the unlettered slave himself, and the multitude around, have long since heard and assented to the decision, is simply to make himself ridiculous. We may be tempted to ask from whom he received his commission, and who he is that received it; what novel statutes he obeys, and what precedents are to him of authority. Such an arbiters very existence is an impertinence. We do not ask him to make up his mind, but to make up his pack.

I listen to hear the voice of a Governor, Commander-in-Chief of the forces of Massachusetts. I hear only the creaking of crickets and the hum of insects which now fill the summer air. The Governor's exploit is to review the troops on muster days. I have seen him on horseback, with his hat off, listening to a chaplain's prayer. It chances that is all I have ever seen of a Governor. I think that I could manage to get along without one. If *he* is not of the least use to prevent my being kidnapped, pray of what important use is he likely to be to me? When freedom is most endangered, he dwells in the deepest obscurity. A distinguished clergyman told me that he chose the profession of a clergyman, because it afforded the most leisure for literary pursuits. I would recommend to him the profession of a Governor.

Three years ago, also, when the Simm's tragedy was acted, I said to myself, there is such an officer, if not such a man, as the Governor of Massachusetts,—what has he been about the last fortnight? Has he had as much as he could do to keep on the fence during this moral earthquake? It seemed to me that no keener satire could have been aimed at, no more cutting insult have been offered to that man, than just what happened—the absence of all inquiry after him in that crisis. The worst and the most I chance to know of him is, that he did not improve that opportunity to make himself known, and worthily known. He could at least have *resigned* himself into fame. It appeared to be forgotten that there was such a man, or such an office. Yet no doubt he was endeavoring to fill the gubernatorial chair all the while. He was no Governor of mine. He did not govern me.

But at last, in the present case, the Governor was heard from. After he and the United States Government had perfectly succeeded in robbing a poor innocent black man of his liberty for life, and, as far as they could, of his Creator's likeness in his breast, he made a speech to his accomplices, at a congratulatory supper!

I have read a recent law of this State, making it penal for 'any officer of the Commonwealth' to 'detain, or aid in the . . . detention,' any where within its limits, 'of any person, for the reason that he is claimed as a fugitive slave.' Also, it was a matter of notoriety that a writ of replevin to take the fugitive out of the custody of the United States Marshal could not be served, for want of sufficient force to aid the officer.

I had thought that the Governor was in some sense the executive officer of the State; that it was his business, as a Governor, to see that the laws of the State were executed; while, as a man, he took care that he did not, by so doing, break the laws of humanity; but when there is any special important use for him, he is useless, or worse than useless, and permits the laws of the State to go unexecuted. Perhaps I do not know what are the duties of a Governor; but if to be a Governor requires to subject one's self to so much ignominy without remedy, if it is to put a restraint upon my manhood, I shall take care never to be Governor of Massachusetts. I have not read far in the statutes of this Commonwealth. It is not profitable reading. They do not always say what is true; and they do not always mean what they say. What I am concerned to know is, that that man's influence and authority were on the side of the slaveholder, and not of the slave—of the guilty, and not of the innocent—of injustice, and not of justice. I never saw him of whom I speak; indeed, I did not know that he was Governor until this event occurred. I heard of him and Anthony Burns at the same time, and thus, undoubtedly, most will hear of him. So far am I from being governed by him. I do not mean that it was any thing to his discredit that I had not heard of him, only that I heard what I did. The worst I shall say of him is, that he proved no better than the majority of his constituents would be likely to prove. In my opinion, he was not equal to the occasion.

The whole military force of the State is at the service of a Mr. Suttle, a slaveholder from Virginia, to enable him to catch a man whom he calls his property; but not a soldier is offered to save a citizen of Massachusetts from being kidnapped! Is this what all these soldiers, all this *training* has been for these seventy-nine years past? Have they been trained merely to rob Mexico, and carry back fugitive slaves to their masters?

These very nights, I heard the sound of a drum in our streets. There were men *training* still; and for what? I could with an effort pardon the cockerels of Concord for crowing still, for they, per-chance, had not been beaten that morning; but I could not excuse this rub-a-dub of the 'trainers.' The slave was carried back by exactly such as these, i.e., by the soldier, of whom the best you can say in this connection is, that he is a fool made conspicuous by a painted coat.

Three years ago, also, just a week after the authorities of Boston assembled to carry back a perfectly innocent man, and one whom they knew to be innocent, into slavery, the inhabitants of Concord caused the bells to be rung and the cannons to be fired, to celebrate their liberty—and the courage and love of liberty of their ancestors who fought at the bridge. As if *those* three millions had fought for the right to be free themselves, but to hold in slavery three millions others. Now-a-days, men wear a fool's cap, and call it a liberty cap. I do not know but there are some, who, if they were tied to a whipping-post, and could get but one hand free, would use it to ring the bells and fire the cannons, to celebrate *their* liberty. So some of my townsmen took the liberty to ring and fire; that was the extent of their freedom; and when the sound of the bells died away, their liberty died away also; when the powder was all expended, their liberty went off with the smoke.

The joke could be no broader, if the inmates of the prisons were to subscribe for all the powder to be used in such salutes, and hire the jailors to do the firing and ringing for them, while they enjoyed it through the grating.

This is what I thought about my neighbors.

Every humane and intelligent inhabitant of Concord, when he or she heard those bells and those cannons, thought not with pride of the events of the 19th of April, 1775, but with shame of the events of the 12th of April, 1851. But now we have half buried that old shame under a new one.

Massachusetts sat waiting Mr. Loring's decision, as if it could in any way affect her own criminality. Her crime, the most conspicuous and fatal crime of all, was permitting him to be the umpire in such a case. It was really the trial of Massachusetts. Every moment that she hesitated to set this man free—every moment that she now hesitates to atone for her crime, she is convicted. The Commissioner on her case is God; not Edward G. God, but simple God.

I wish my countrymen to consider, that whatever the human law may be, neither an individual nor a nation can ever commit the least act of injustice against the obscurest individual, without having to pay the penalty for it. A government which deliberately enacts injustice, and persists in it, will at length ever become the laughing-stock of the world. Much has been said about American slavery, but I think that we do not even yet realize what slavery is. If I were seriously to propose to Congress to make mankind into sausages, I have no doubt that most of the members would smile at my proposition, and if any believed me to be in earnest, they would think that I proposed something much worse than Congress had ever done. But if any of them will tell me that to make a man into a sausage would be much worse,—would be any worse, than to make him into a slave,—than it was to enact the Fugitive Slave Law, I will accuse him of foolishness, of intellectual incapacity, of making a distinction without a difference. The one is just as reasonable a proposition as the other.

I hear a good deal said about trampling this law under foot. Why, one need not go out of his way to do that. This law rises not to the level of the head or the reason; its natural habitat is in the dirt. It was born and bred, and has its life only in the dust and mire, on a level with the feet, and he who walks with freedom, and does not with Hindoo mercy avoid treading on every venomous reptile, will inevitably tread on it, and so trample it under foot,—and Webster, its maker, with it, like the dirt-bug and its ball.

Recent events will be valuable as a criticism on the administration of justice in our midst, or, rather, as showing what are the true resources of justice in any community. It has come to this, that the friends of liberty, the friends of the slave, have shuddered when they have understood that his fate was left to the legal tribunals of the country to be decided. Free men have no faith that justice will be awarded in such a case; the judge may decide this way or that; it is a kind of accident, at best. It is evident that he is not a competent authority in so important a case. It is no time, then, to be judging according to his precedents, but to establish a precedent for the future. I would much rather trust to the sentiment of the people. In their vote, you would get something of some value, at least, however small; but, in the other case, only the trammelled judgment of an individual, of no significance, be it which way it might.

It is to some extent fatal to the courts, when the people are compelled to go behind them. I do not wish to believe that the courts were made for fair weather, and for very civil cases merely,—but think of leaving it to any court in the land to decide whether more than three millions of people, in this case, a sixth part of a nation, have a right to be freemen or not! But it has been left to the courts of *justice,* so-called—to the Supreme Court of the land—and, as you all know, recognizing no authority but the Constitution, it has decided that the three millions are, and shall continue to be, slaves. Such judges as these are merely the inspectors of a pick-lock and murderer's tools, to tell him whether they are in working order or not, and there they think that their responsibility ends. There was a prior case on the docket, which they, as judges appointed by God, had no right to skip; which having been justly settled, they would have been saved from this humiliation. It was the case of the murderer himself.

The law will never make men free; it is men who have got to make the law free. They are the lovers of law and order, who observe the law when the government breaks it.

Among human beings, the judge whose words seal the fate of a man furthest into eternity, is not he who merely pronounces the verdict of the law, but he, whoever he may be, who, from a love of truth, and unprejudiced by any custom or enactment of men, utters a true opinion or *sentence* concerning him. He it is that *sentences* him. Whoever has discerned truth, has received his commission from a higher source than the chiefest justice in the world, who can discern only law. He finds himself constituted judge of the judge.—Strange that it should be necessary to state such simple truths.

I am more and more convinced that, with reference to any public question, it is more important to know what the country thinks of it, than what the city thinks. The city does not *think* much. On any moral question, I would rather have the opinion of Boxboro than of Boston and New York put together. When the former speaks, I feel as if somebody *had* spoken, as if *humanity* was yet, and a reasonable being had asserted its rights,—as if some unprejudiced men among the country's hills had at length turned their attention to the subject, and by a few sensible words redeemed the reputation of the race. When, in some obscure country town, the farmers come together to a special town meeting, to express their opinion on some subject which is vexing the land, that, I think, is the true Congress, and the most respectable one that is ever assembled in the United States.

It is evident that there are, in this Commonwealth, at least, two parties, becoming more and more distinct—the party of the city, and the party of the country. I know that the country is mean enough, but I am glad to believe that there is a slight difference in her favor. But as yet, she has few, if any organs, through which to express herself. The editorials which she reads, like the news, come from the sea-board. Let us, the inhabitants of the country, cultivate self-respect. Let us not send to the city for aught more essential than our broadcloths and groceries, or, if we read the opinions of the city, let us entertain opinions of our own.

Among measures to be adopted, I would suggest to make as earnest and vigorous an assault on the Press as has already been made, and with effect, on the Church. The Church has much improved within a few years; but the Press is almost, without exception, corrupt. I believe that, in this country, the press exerts a greater and a more pernicious influence than the Church did in its worst period. We are not a religious people, but we are a nation of politicians. We do not care for the Bible, but we do care for the newspaper. At any meeting of politicians,—like that at Concord the other evening, for instance,—how impertinent it would be to quote from the Bible! how pertinent to quote from a newspaper or from the Constitution! The newspaper is a Bible which we read every morning and every afternoon, standing and sitting, riding and walking. It is a Bible which every man carries in his pocket, which lies on every table and counter, and which the mail, and thousands of missionaries, are continually dispensing. It is, in short, the only book which America has printed, and which America reads. So wide is its influence. The editor is a preacher whom you voluntarily support. Your tax is commonly one cent daily, and it costs nothing for pew hire. But how many of these preachers preach the truth? I repeat the testimony of many an intelligent foreigner, as well as my own convictions, when I say, that probably no country was ever ruled by so mean a class of tyrants as, with a few noble exceptions, are the editors of the periodical press in *this* country. And as they live and rule only by their servility, and appealing to the worst, and not the better nature of man, the people who read them are in the condition of the dog that returns to his vomit.

The *Liberator* and the *Commonwealth* were the only papers in Boston, as far as I know, which made themselves heard in condemnation of the cowardice and meanness of the authorities of that city, as exhibited in '51. The other journals, almost without exception, by their manner of referring to and speaking of the Fugitive Slave Law, and the carrying back of the slave Simms, insulted the common sense of the country, at least. And, for the most part, they did this, one would say, because they thought so to secure the approbation of their patrons, not being aware that a sounder sentiment prevailed to any extent in the heart of the Commonwealth. I am told that some of them have improved of late; but they are still eminently time-serving. Such is the character they have won.

But, thank fortune, this preacher can be even more easily reached by the weapons of the reformer than could the recreant priest. The free men of New England have only to refrain from purchasing and reading these sheets, have only to withhold their cents, to kill a score of them at once. One whom I respect told me that he purchased Mitchell's *Citizen* in the cars, and then threw it out the window. But would not his contempt have been more fatally expressed, if he had not bought it?

Are they Americans? are they New Englanders? are they inhabitants of Lexington, and Concord, and Framingham, who read and support the Boston *Post, Mail, Journal, Advertiser, Courier,* and *Times?* Are these the Flags of our Union? I am not a newspaper reader, and may omit to name the worst.

Could slavery suggest a more complete servility than some of these journals exhibit? Is there any dust which their conduct does not lick, and make fouler still with its slime? I do not know whether the Boston *Herald* is still in existence, but I remember to have seen it about the streets when Simms was carried off. Did it not act its part well—serve its master faithfully? How could it have gone lower on its belly? How can a man stoop lower than he is low? do more than put his extremities in the place of the head he has? than make his head his lower extremity? When I have taken up this paper with my cuffs turned up, I have heard the gurgling of the sewer through every column. I have felt that I was handling a paper picked out of the public gutters, a leaf from the gospel of the gambling-house, the groggery and the brothel, harmonizing with the gospel of the Merchants' Exchange.

The majority of the men of the North, and of the South, and East, and West, are not men of principle. If they vote, they do not send men to Congress on errands of humanity, but while their brothers and sisters are being scourged and hung for loving liberty, while—I might here insert all that slavery implies and is,—it is the mismanagement of wood and iron and stone and gold which concerns them. Do what you will, O Government! with my wife and children, my mother and brother, my father and sister, I will obey your commands to the letter. It will indeed grieve me if you hurt them, if you deliver them to overseers to be hunted by hounds or to be whipped to death; but nevertheless, I will peaceably pursue my chosen calling on this fair earth, until perchance, one day, when I have put on mourning for them dead, I shall have persuaded you to relent. Such is the attitude, such are the words of Massachusetts.

Rather than do thus, I need not say what match I would touch, what system endeavor to blow up,—but as I love my life, I would side with the light, and let the dark earth roll from under me, calling my mother and my brother to follow.

I would remind my countrymen, that they are to be men first, and Americans only at a late and convenient hour. No matter how valuable law may be to protect your property, even to keep soul and body together, if it do not keep you and humanity together.

I am sorry to say, that I doubt if there is a judge in Massachusetts who is prepared to resign his office, and get his living innocently, whenever it is required of him to pass sentence under a law which is merely contrary to the law of God. I am compelled to see that they put themselves, or rather, are by character, in this respect, exactly on a level with the marine who discharges his musket in any direction he is ordered to. They are just as much tools and as little men. Certainly, they are not the more to be respected, because their master enslaves their understandings and consciences, instead of their bodies.

The judges and lawyers,—simply as such, I mean,—and all men of expediency, try this case by a very low and incompetent standard.

They consider, not whether the Fugitive Slave Law is right, but whether it is what they call *constitutional*. Is virtue constitutional, or vice? Is equity constitutional, or iniquity? In important moral and vital questions like this, it is just as impertinent to ask whether a law is constitutional or not, as to ask whether it is profitable or not. They persist in being the servants of the worst of men, and not the servants of humanity. The question is not whether you or your grandfather, seventy years ago, did not enter into an agreement to serve the devil, and that service is not accordingly now due; but whether you will not now, for once and at last, serve God,—in spite of your own past recreancy, or that of your ancestor,—by obeying that eternal and only just CONSTITUTION, which He, and not any Jefferson or Adams, has written in your being.

The amount of it is, if the majority vote the devil to be God, the minority will live and behave accordingly, trusting that some time or other, by some Speaker's casting vote, perhaps, they may reinstate God. This is the highest principle I can get out of or invent for my neighbors. These men act as if they believed that they could safely slide down hill a little way—or a good way—and would surely come to a place, by and by, where they could begin to slide up again. This is expediency, or choosing that course which offers the slightest obstacles to the feet, that is, a downhill one. But there is no such thing as accomplishing a righteous reform by the use of 'expediency.' There is no such thing as sliding up hill. In morals, the only sliders are backsliders.

Thus we steadily worship Mammon, both School, and State, and Church, and the Seventh Day curse God with a tintamar from one end of the Union to the other.

Will mankind never learn that policy is not morality—that it never secures any moral right, but considers merely what is expedient? chooses the available candidate, who is invariably the devil,—and what right have his constituents to be surprised, because the devil does not behave like an angel of light? What is wanted is men, not of policy, but of probity—who recognize a higher law than the Constitution, or the decision of the majority. The fate of the country does not depend on how you vote at the polls—the worst man is as strong as the best at that game; it does not depend on what kind of paper you drop into the ballot-box once a year, but on what kind of man you drop from your chamber into the street every morning.

What should concern Massachusetts is not the Nebraska Bill, nor the Fugitive Slave Bill, but her own slaveholding and servility. Let the State dissolve her union with the slaveholder. She may wriggle and hesitate, and ask leave to read the Constitution once more; but she can find no respectable law or precedent which sanctions the continuance of such a Union for an instant.

Let each inhabitant of the State dissolve his union with her, as long as she delays to do her duty.

The events of the past month teach me to distrust Fame. I see that she does not finely discriminate, but coarsely hurrahs. She considers not the simple heroism of an action, but only as it is connected with its apparent consequences. She praises till she is hoarse the easy exploit of the Boston tea party, but will be comparatively silent about the braver and more disinterestedly heroic attack on the Boston Court-House, simply because it was unsuccessful!

Covered with disgrace, the State has sat down coolly to try for their lives and liberties the men who attempted to do its duty for it. And this is called *justice!* They who have shown that they can behave particularly well may perchance be put under bonds for *their good behavior.* They whom truth requires at present to plead guilty, are of all the inhabitants of the State, preeminently innocent. While the Governor, and the Mayor, and countless officers of the Commonwealth, are at large, the champions of liberty are imprisoned.

Only they are guiltless, who commit the crime of contempt of such a Court. It behoves every man to see that his influence is on the side of justice, and let the courts make their own characters. My sympathies in this case are wholly with the accused, and wholly against the accusers and their judges. Justice is sweet and musical; but injustice is harsh and discordant. The judge still sits grinding at his organ, but it yields no music, and we hear only the sound of the handle. He believes that all the music resides in the handle, and the crowd toss him their coppers the same as before.

Do you suppose that that Massachusetts which is now doing these things,—which hesitates to crown these men, some of whose lawyers, and even judges, perchance, may be driven to take refuge in some poor quibble, that they may not wholly outrage their instinctive sense of justice,—do you suppose that she is any thing but base and servile? that she is the champion of liberty?

Show me a free State, and a court truly of justice, and I will fight for them, if need be; but show me Massachusetts, and I refuse her my allegiance, and express contempt for her courts.

The effect of a good government is to make life more valuable,— of a bad one, to make it less valuable. We can afford that railroad, and all other merely material stock, should lose some of its value, for that only compels us to live more simply and economically; but suppose that the value of life itself should be diminished! How can we make a less demand on man and nature, how live more economically in respect to virtue and all noble qualities, than we do? I have lived for the last month,—and I think that every man in Massachusetts capable of the sentiment of patriotism must have had a similar experience,—with the sense of having suffered a vast and indefinite loss. I did not know at first what ailed me. At last it occurred to me that what I had lost was a country. I had never respected the Government near to which I had lived, but I had foolishly thought that I might manage to live here, minding my private affairs, and forget it. For my part, my old and worthiest pursuits have lost I cannot say how much of their attraction, and I feel that my investment in life here is worth many per cent. less since Massachusetts last deliberately sent back an innocent man, Anthony Burns, to slavery. I dwelt before, perhaps, in the illusion that my life passed somewhere only *between* heaven and hell, but now I cannot persuade myself that I do not dwell *wholly within* hell. The site of that political organization called Massachusetts is to me morally covered with volcanic scoriæ and cinders, such as Milton describes in the infernal regions. If there is any hell more unprincipled than our rulers, and we, the ruled, I feel curious to see it. Life itself being worth less, all things with it, which minister to it, are worth less. Suppose you have a small library, with pictures to adorn the walls—a garden laid out around—and contemplate scientific and literary pursuits, &c, and discover all at once that your villa, with all its contents, is located in hell, and that the justice of the peace has a cloven foot and a forked tail—do not these things suddenly lose their value in your eyes?

I feel that, to some extent, the State has fatally interfered in my lawful business. It has not only interrupted me in my passage through Court street on errands of trade, but it has interrupted me and every man on his onward and upward path, on which he had trusted soon to leave Court street far behind. What right had it to remind me of Court street? I have found that hollow which even I had relied on for solid.

I am surprised to see men going about their business as if nothing had happened. I say to myself—Unfortunates! they have not heard the news. I am surprised that the man whom I just met on horseback should be so earnest to overtake his newly-bought cows running away—since all property is insecure—and if they do not run away again, they may be taken away from him when he gets them. Fool! does he not know that his seed-corn is worth less this year—that all beneficent harvests fail as you approach the empire of hell? No prudent man will build a store-house under these circumstances, or engage in any peaceful enterprise which requires a long time to accomplish. Art is as long as ever, but life is more interrupted and less available for a man's proper pursuits. It is not an era of repose. We have used up all our inherited freedom. If we would save our lives, we must fight for them.

I walk toward one of our ponds, but what signifies the beauty of nature when men are base? We walk to lakes to see our serenity reflected in them; when we are not serene, we go not to them. Who can be serene in a country where both the rulers and the ruled are without principle? The remembrance of my country spoils my walk. My thoughts are murder to the State, and involuntarily go plotting against her.

But it chanced the other day that I secured a white water-lily, and a season I had waited for had arrived. It is the emblem of purity. It bursts up so pure and fair to the eye, and so sweet to the scent, as if to show us what purity and sweetness reside in, and can be extracted from, the slime and muck of earth. I think I have plucked the first one that has opened for a mile. What confirmation of our hopes is in the fragrance of this flower! I shall not so soon despair of the world for it, notwithstanding slavery, and the cowardice and want of principle of Northern men. It suggests what kind of laws have prevailed longest and widest, and still prevail, and that the time may come when man's deeds may smell as sweet. Such is the odor which the plant emits. If Nature can compound this fragrance still annually, I shall believe her still young and full of vigor, her integrity and genius unimpaired, and that there is virtue even in man, too, who is fitted to perceive and love it. It reminds me that Nature has been partner to no Missouri Compromise. I scent no compromise in the fragrance of the water-lily. It is not a *Nymphoea Douglassii*. In it, the sweet, and pure, and innocent, are wholly sundered from the obscene and baleful. I do not scent in this the time-serving irresolution of a Massachusetts Governor, nor of a Boston Mayor. So behave that the odor of your actions may enhance the general sweetness of the atmosphere, that when we behold or scent a flower, we may not be reminded how inconsistent your deeds are with it; for all odor is but one form of advertisement of a moral quality, and if fair actions had not been performed, the lily would not smell sweet. The foul slime stands for the sloth and vice of man, the decay of humanity; the fragrant flower that springs from it, for the purity and courage which are immortal.

Slavery and servility have produced no sweet-scented flower annually, to charm the senses of men, for they have no real life: they are merely a decaying and a death, offensive to all healthy nostrils. We do not complain that they *live,* but that they do not *get buried.* Let the living bury them; even they are good for manure.

LEO TOLSTOY

"Repent ye, for the Kingdom of Heaven is at Hand" (1893)

Translated by Constance Garnett

The great Russian novelist (1828–1910) had a major religious awakening after a difficult and despairing decade in the 1870s, during which he wrote one of the most glorious novels in world literature, Anna Karenina. *He could not help discovering in his study of the New Testament that the Russian Orthodox Church was promoting an unchristian Christianity, and by the early 1880s Tolstoy had committed himself to pacifism and a strict adherence to Christ's law of nonresistance. He wrote several influential and popular books about social reform through civil disobedience and the application of Christ's teachings, for which he was excommunicated. With his international fame as a novelist, he was able to avoid arrest and persist in his writing and to communicate his ideas to worldwide readers. Perhaps his grandest of religious-political works,* The Kingdom of God is Within You, *is as much a history of an idea as it is a brilliant argument for "nonaction." The Tolstoy scholar Michael Denner observes: "Near the end of* The Kingdom of God is Within You *[...] he advocates nonaction as a revolutionary means, noting that every government has the means to defend itself from revolutionaries and their violent modus operandi. But what can a government do, Tolstoy asks, against men who declaim against all authority as useless and superfluous but who offer no opposition, merely rejecting the government's offices and services, refusing to participate in it?"[1] I have excerpted the first section of his hundred-page "Conclusion," wherein Tolstoy, aghast, describes how nonviolent civil obedience has resulted in the government's "legal" hanging of peasants: "This is what has often been done in Russia, and is and must always be done where the social order is based on force."*

---

[1] Michael Denner. "Tolstoyan Nonaction: The Advantage of Doing Nothing." *Tolstoy Studies Journal.* Volume XIII. Toronto: Tolstoy Society. 2001. 18.

CHANCE MEETING WITH a Train Carrying Soldiers to Restore Order Among the Famishing Peasants—Reason of the Expedition—How the Decisions of the Higher Authorities are Enforced in Cases of Insubordination on Part of the Peasants—What Happened at Orel, as an Example of How the Rights of the Propertied Classes are Maintained by Murder and Torture—All the Privileges of the Wealthy are Based on Similar Acts of Violence.

I was finishing this book, which I had been working at for two years, when I happened on the 9th of September to be traveling by rail through the governments of Toula and Riazan, where the peasants were starving last year and where the famine is even more severe now. At one of the railway stations my train passed an extra train which was taking a troop of soldiers under the conduct of the governor of the province, together with muskets, cartridges, and rods, to flog and murder these same famishing peasants.

The punishment of flogging by way of carrying the decrees of the authorities into effect has been more and more frequently adopted of late in Russia, in spite of the fact that corporal punishment was abolished by law thirty years ago.

I had heard of this, I had even read in the newspapers of the fearful floggings which had been inflicted in Tchernigov, Tambov, Saratov, Astrakhan, and Orel, and of those of which the governor of Nijni-Novgorod, General Baranov, had boasted. But I had never before happened to see men in the process of carrying out these punishments.

And here I saw the spectacle of good Russians full of the Christian spirit traveling with guns and rods to torture and kill their starving brethren. The reason for their expedition was as follows:

On one of the estates of a rich landowner the peasants had common rights on the forest, and having always enjoyed these rights, regarded the forest as their own, or at least as theirs in common with the owner. The landowner wished to keep the forest entirely to himself and began to fell the trees. The peasants lodged a complaint. The judges in the first instance gave an unjust decision (I say unjust on the authority of the lawyer and governor, who ought to understand the matter), and decided the case in favor of the landowner. All the later decisions, even that of the senate, though they could see that the matter had been unjustly decided, confirmed the judgment and adjudged the forest to the landowner. He began to cut down the trees, but the peasants, unable to believe that such obvious injustice could be done them by the higher authorities, did not submit to the decision and drove away the men sent to cut down the trees, declaring that the forest belonged to them and they would go to the Tzar before they would let them cut it down.

The matter was referred to Petersburg, and the order was transmitted to the governor to carry the decision of the court into effect. The governor asked for a troop of soldiers. And here were the soldiers with bayonets and cartridges, and moreover, a supply of rods, expressly prepared for the purpose and heaped up in one of the trucks, going to carry the decision of the higher authorities into effect.

The decisions of the higher authorities are carried into effect by means of murder or torture, or threats of one or the other, according to whether they offer resistance or not.

In the first case if the peasants offer resistance the practice is in Russia, and it is the same everywhere where a state organization and private property exist, as follows. The governor delivers an address in which he demands submission. The excited crowd, generally deluded by their leaders, don't understand a word of what the representative of authority is saying in the pompous official language, and their excitement continues. Then the governor announces that if they do not submit and disperse, he will be obliged to have recourse to force. If the crowd does not disperse even on this, the governor gives the order to fire over the heads of the crowd. If the crowd does not even then disperse, the governor gives the order to fire straight into the crowd; the soldiers fire and the killed and wounded fall about the street. Then the crowd usually runs away in all directions, and the troops at the governor's command take those who are supposed to be the ringleaders and lead them off under escort. Then they pick up the dying, the wounded, and the dead, covered with blood, sometimes women and children among them. The dead they bury and the wounded they carry to the hospital. Those whom they regard as the ringleaders they take to the town hall and have them tried by a special court-martial. And if they have had recourse to violence on their side, they are condemned to be hanged. And then the gallows is erected. And they solemnly strangle a few defenseless creatures.

This is what has often been done in Russia, and is and must always be done where the social order is based on force.

But in the second case, when the peasants do submit, something quite special, peculiar to Russia, takes place. The governor arrives on the scene of action and delivers an harangue to the people, reproaching them for their insubordination, and either stations troops in the houses of the villages, where sometimes for a whole month the soldiers drain the resources of the peasants, or contenting himself with threats, he mercifully takes leave of the people, or what is the most frequent course, he announces that the ringleaders must be punished, and quite arbitrarily without any trial selects a certain number of men, regarded as ringleaders, and commands them to be flogged in his presence.

In order to give an idea of how such things are done I will describe a proceeding of the kind which took place in Orel, and received the full approval of the highest authorities.

This is what took place in Orel. Just as here in the Toula province, a landlord wanted to appropriate the property of the peasants and just in the same way the peasants opposed it. The matter in dispute was a fall of water, which irrigated the peasants' fields, and which the landowner wanted to cut off and divert to turn his mill. The peasants rebelled against this being done. The land owner laid a complaint before the district commander, who illegally (as was recognized later even by a legal decision) decided the matter in favor of the landowner, and allowed him to divert the water course. The landowner sent workmen to dig the conduit by which the water was to be let off to turn the mill. The peasants were indignant at this unjust decision, and sent their women to prevent the landowner's men from digging this conduit. The women went to the dykes, overturned the carts, and drove away the men. The landowner made a complaint against the women for thus taking the law into their own hands. The district commander made out an order that from every house throughout the village one woman was to be taken and put in prison. The order was not easily executed. For in every household there were several women, and it was impossible to know which one was to be arrested. Consequently the police did not carry out the order. The landowner complained to the governor of the neglect on the part of the police, and the latter, without examining into the affair, gave the chief official of the police strict orders to carry out the instructions of the district commander without delay. The police official, in obedience to his superior, went to the village and with the insolence peculiar to Russian officials ordered his policemen to take one woman out of each house. But since there were more than one woman in each house, and there was no knowing which one was sentenced to imprisonment, disputes and opposition arose. In spite of these disputes and opposition, however, the officer of police gave orders that some woman, whichever came first, should be taken from each household and led away to prison. The peasants began to defend their wives and mothers, would not let them go, and beat the police and their officer. This was a fresh and terrible crime: resistance was offered to the authorities. A report of this new offense was sent to the town. And so this governor—precisely as the governor of Toula was doing on that day—with a battalion of soldiers with guns and rods, hastily brought together by means of telegraphs and telephones and railways, proceeded by a special train to the scene of action, with a learned doctor whose duty it was to insure the flogging being of an hygienic character. Herzen's prophecy of the modern Genghis Khan with his telegrams is completely realized by this governor.

Before the town hall of the district were the soldiery, a battalion of police with their revolvers slung round them with red cords, the persons of most importance among the peasants, and the culprits. A crowd of one thousand or more people were standing round. The governor, on arriving, stepped out of his carriage, delivered a prepared harangue, and asked for the culprits and a bench. The latter demand was at first not understood. But a police constable whom the governor always took about with him, and who undertook to organize such executions—by no means exceptional in that province—explained that what was meant was a bench for flogging. A bench was brought as well as the rods, and then the executioners were summoned (the latter had been selected beforehand from some horsestealers of the same village, as the soldiers refused the office). When everything was ready, the governor ordered the first of the twelve culprits pointed out by the landowner as the most guilty to come forward. The first to come forward was the head of a family, a man of forty who had always stood up manfully for the rights of his class, and therefore was held in the greatest esteem by all the villagers. He was led to the bench and stripped, and then ordered to lie down.

The peasant attempted to supplicate for mercy, but seeing it was useless, he crossed himself and lay down. Two police constables hastened to hold him down. The learned doctor stood by, in readiness to give his aid and his medical science when they should be needed. The convicts spit into their hands, brandished the rods, and began to flog. It seemed, however, that the bench was too narrow, and it was difficult to keep the victim writhing in torture upon

it. Then the governor ordered them to bring another bench and to
put a plank across them. Soldiers, with their hands raised to their
caps, and respectful murmurs of "Yes, your Excellency," hasten
obediently to carry out this order. Meanwhile the tortured man,
half naked, pale and scowling, stood waiting, his eyes fixed on the
ground and his teeth chattering. When another bench had been
brought they again made him lie down, and the convicted thieves
again began to flog him.

The victim's back and thighs and legs, and even his sides, became
more and more covered with scars and wheals, and at every blow
there came the sound of the deep groans which he could no longer
restrain. In the crowd standing round were heard the sobs of wives,
mothers, children, the families of the tortured man and of all the
others picked out for punishment.

The miserable governor, intoxicated with power, was counting
the strokes on his fingers, and never left off smoking cigarettes,
while several officious persons hastened on every opportunity to
offer him a burning match to light them. When more than fifty
strokes had been given, the peasant ceased to shriek and writhe, and
the doctor, who had been educated in a government institution to
serve his sovereign and his country with his scientific attainments,
went up to the victim, felt his pulse, listened to his heart, and
announced to the representative of authority that the man under-
going punishment had lost consciousness, and that, in accordance
with the conclusions of science, to continue the punishment would
endanger the victim's life. But the miserable governor, now completely intoxicated by the sight of blood, gave orders that the punishment should go on, and the flogging was continued up to
seventy strokes, the number which the governor had for some
reason fixed upon as necessary. When the seventieth stroke had
been reached, the governor said "Enough! Next one!" And the
mutilated victim, his back covered with blood, was lifted up and
carried away unconscious, and another was led up. The sobs and
groans of the crowd grew louder. But the representative of the state
continued the torture.

Thus they flogged each of them up to the twelfth, and each of
them received seventy strokes. They all implored mercy, shrieked
and groaned. The sobs and cries of the crowd of women grew
louder and more heart-rending, and the men's faces grew darker
and darker. But they were surrounded by troops, and the torture
did not cease till it had reached the limit which had been fixed by

the caprice of the miserable half-drunken and insane creature they called the governor.

The officials, and officers, and soldiers not only assisted in it, but were even partly responsible for the affair, since by their presence they prevented any interference on the part of the crowd.

When I inquired of one of the governors why they made use of this kind of torture when people had already submitted and soldiers were stationed in the village, he replied with the important air of a man who thoroughly understands all the subtleties of statecraft, that if the peasants were not thoroughly subdued by flogging, they would begin offering opposition to the decisions of authorities again. When some of them had been thoroughly tortured, the authority of the state would be secured forever among them.

And so that was why the Governor of Toula was going in his turn with his subordinate officials, officers, and soldiers to carry out a similar measure. By precisely the same means, i. e., by murder and torture, obedience to the decision of the higher authorities was to be secured. And this decision was to enable a young landowner, who had an income of one hundred thousand, to gain three thousand rubles more by stealing a forest from a whole community of cold and famished peasants, to spend it, in two or three weeks in the saloons of Moscow, Petersburg, or Paris. That was what those people whom I met were going to do.

After my thoughts had for two years been turned in the same direction, fate seemed expressly to have brought me face to face for the first time in my life with a fact which showed me absolutely unmistakably in practice what had long been clear to me in theory, that the organization of our society rests, not as people interested in maintaining the present order of things like to imagine, on certain principles of jurisprudence, but on simple brute force, on the murder and torture of men.

People who own great estates or fortunes, or who receive great revenues drawn from the class who are in want even of necessities, the working class, as well as all those who like merchants, doctors, artists, clerks, learned professors, coachmen, cooks, writers, valets, and barristers, make their living about these rich people, like to believe that the privileges they enjoy are not the result of force, but of absolutely free and just interchange of services, and that their advantages, far from being gained by such punishments and murders as took place in Orel and several parts of Russia this year, and are always taking place all over Europe and America, have no kind of connection with these acts of violence. They like to believe that their privileges exist apart and are the result of free contract among people; and that the violent cruelties perpetrated on the people also exist apart and are the result of some general judicial, political, or economical laws. They try not to see that they all enjoy their privileges as a result of the same fact which forces the peasants who have tended the forest, and who are in the direct need of it for fuel, to give it up to a rich landowner who has taken no part in caring for its growth and has no need of it whatever—the fact, that is, that if they don't give it up they will be flogged or killed.

And yet if it is clear that it was only by means of menaces, blows, or murder, that the mill in Orel was enabled to yield a larger income, or that the forest which the peasants had planted became the property of a landowner, it should be equally clear that all the other exclusive rights enjoyed by the rich, by robbing the poor of their necessities, rest on the same basis of violence. If the peasants, who need land to maintain their families, may not cultivate the land about their houses, but one man, a Russian, English, Austrian, or any other great land-owner, possesses land enough to maintain a thousand families, though he does not cultivate it himself, and if a merchant profiting by the misery of the cultivators, taking corn from them at a third of its value, can keep this corn in his granaries with perfect security while men are starving all around him, and sell it again for three times its value to the very cultivators he bought it from, it is evident that all this too comes from the same cause. And if one man may not buy of another a commodity from the other side of a certain fixed line, called the frontier, without paying certain duties on it to men who have taken no part whatever in its production—and if men are driven to sell their last cow to pay taxes which the government distributes among its functionaries, and spends on maintaining soldiers to murder these very taxpayers it would appear self-evident that all this does not come about as the result of any abstract laws, but is based on just what was done in Orel, and which may be done in Toula, and is done peri-odically in one form or another throughout the whole world wher-ever there is a government, and where there are rich and poor.

Simply because torture and murder are not employed in every instance of oppression by force, those who enjoy the exclusive privileges of the ruling classes persuade themselves and others that their privileges are not based on torture and murder, but on some mysterious general causes, abstract laws, and so on. Yet one would think it was perfectly clear that if men, who consider it unjust (and all the working classes do consider it so nowadays), still pay the principal part of the produce of their labor away to the capitalist and the landowner, and pay taxes, though they know to what a bad use these taxes are put, they do so not from recognition of abstract laws of which they have never heard, but only because they know they will be beaten and killed if they don't do so.

And if there is no need to imprison, beat, and kill men every time the landlord collects his rents, every time those who are in want of bread have to pay a swindling merchant three times its value, every time the factory hand has to be content with a wage less than half of the profit made by the employer, and every time a poor man pays his last ruble in taxes, it is because so many men have been beaten and killed for trying to resist these demands, that the lesson has now been learnt very thoroughly.

Just as a trained tiger, who does not eat meat put under his nose, and jumps over a stick at the word of command, does not act thus because he likes it, but because he remembers the red-hot irons or the fast with which he was punished every time he did not obey; so men submitting to what is disadvantageous or even ruinous to them, and considered by them as unjust, act thus because they remember what they suffered for resisting it.

As for those who profit by the privileges gained by previous acts of violence, they often forget and like to forget how these privileges were obtained. But one need only recall the facts of history, not the history of the exploits of different dynasties of rulers, but real history, the history of the oppression of the majority by a small number of men, to see that all the advantages the rich have over the poor are based on nothing but flogging, imprisonment, and murder.

One need but reflect on the unceasing, persistent struggle of all to better their material position, which is the guiding motive of men of the present day, to be convinced that the advantages of the rich over the poor could never and can never be maintained by anything but force.

There may be cases of oppression, of violence, and of punishments, though they are rare, the aim of which is not to secure the privileges of the propertied classes. But one may confidently assert that in any society where, for every man living in ease, there are ten exhausted by labor, envious, covetous, and often suffering with their families from direct privation, all the privileges of the rich, all their luxuries and superfluities, are obtained and maintained only by tortures, imprisonment, and murder.

LEO TOLSTOY

Two Wars (1898)

Tolstoy reflects, from his home at Yasnaya Polyana, on the recently ended "stupid, cruel" Spanish-American War in contrast to "the war against war." He hails, among others, the religious sect in Russia known as the Dukhobors, who, persecuted by the Russian government, exhibiting the purest form of civil disobedience, "put forth nothing but their own religious instrument, meek reasonableness and long-suffering firmness, and say: 'We must not obey men more than God, and no matter what they may do, we cannot and will not obey them.'" After several examples of men obeying Christ's words of pacifism, Tolstoy concludes: "The weapon is, for each man to follow his own reason and conscience."

TWO WARS ARE at the present time being waged in the Christian world. One, it is true, has been ended, while the other is still going on; but they were waged at one and the same time, and the contrast between the two is striking. The first, now ended, was an old, vainglorious, stupid, cruel, untimely, obsolete, pagan war, the Spanish-American War, which by the murder of one set of men decided how and by whom another set of men was to be ruled. The second war, which is still going on, and which will be ended only when all wars shall end, is a new, self-sacrificing, sacred war, which is based on nothing but love and reason, the war against war, which (as Victor Hugo expressed it at one of the congresses) the best, most advanced part of the Christian humanity declared long ago against the other, the coarse and savage part of the same humanity, and which a handful of Christian men, the Dukhobors of the Caucasus, have of late waged with particular force and success against the powerful Russian government.

The other day I received a letter from Colorado, from a Mr. Jesse Glodwin, who asks me to send him "a few words or thoughts, expressive of my sentiments, in regard to the noble work of the

66

American nation and the heroism of her soldiers and sailors." This gentleman is, with the vast majority of the American nation, fully convinced that the action of the Americans, which is, that they beat a few thousands of almost unarmed men (in comparison with the armament of the Americans the Spaniards were almost unarmed), is unquestionably a "noble work," and that those people who, having killed a large number of their neighbours, for the most part survived and were well and fixed themselves comfortably in life, were heroes.

The Spanish-American War, to say nothing of the horrible things which the Spaniards had done in Cuba, and which served as the pretext for the war, resembles this:

A decrepit and doting old man, who was brought up in the traditions of false honour, to settle a misunderstanding that arose between him and a young man, challenges this young man, who is in the full possession of his strength, to fisticuffs; and the young man, who, to judge from his past and from what he has said more than once, ought to stand incomparably higher than such a settlement of the question, accepts the challenge with knuckles in his clenched fist, jumps upon the decrepit and doting old man, knocks out his teeth, breaks his ribs, and then ecstatically tells his exploits to a vast public of just such young men as he is, and this public rejoices and praises the hero who has maimed the old man.

Such is the one war which occupied the minds of all in the Christian world. Nobody speaks of the other war; hardly any one knows anything about it. The other war is like this:

All the states deceive the people, saying: "All of you who are ruled by me are in danger of being conquered by other nations; I look after your well-being and security, and so demand that you shall annually give me millions of roubles, the fruits of your labours, which I am going to use for rifles, cannon, powder, ships for your defence; I demand, besides, that you shall enter the organizations instituted by me, where they will make of you senseless particles of an immense machine,—the army,—which I manage. While connected with this army you will cease being men and having your own will, but will do everything I want you to do. What I want to do first of all is to rule, and the means I use for ruling is murder; and so I am going to teach you to commit murder."

In spite of the obvious insipidity of the assertion that men are in danger from the attack of the governments of other states, which assert that they, in spite of their desire for peace, are in the same danger; in spite of the degradation of that slavery to which men are subjected when they enter the army; in spite of the cruelty of the business to which they are called, men submit to the deception, give up their money for their own enslavement, and themselves enslave one another.

And here there appear people who say:

"What you say of the threatening danger and of your concern about protecting us against it is a deception. All the states affirm that they want peace, and at the same time arm themselves against one another. Besides, according to the law which you profess, all men are brothers, and it makes no difference whether we belong to this state or to another, and so the attack of other states upon us, with which you frighten us, has no terror and no meaning for us. But the main thing is this, that, according to the law which was given to us by God, and which you, too, profess, who demand of us a participation in murder, we are clearly forbidden to commit murder or even any acts of violence, and so we cannot and will not take part in your preparations for murder, will not give you any money for the purpose, and will not join the gangs established by you, where you corrupt the reason and the conscience of men, by changing them into instruments of violence, who are submissive to every evil man taking this instrument into his hands."

In this consists the second war, which has for a long time been waged with the representatives of rude force, and which of late has burned up with particular virulence between the Dukhobors and the Russian government. The Russian government has brought out against the Dukhobors all those instruments with which it can fight. These instruments are: the police measures of arrests, the prohibition of leaving the place of abode, the prohibition of intercommunication, the seizure of letters, espionage, the prohibition of printing in the newspapers any information on matters pertaining to the Dukhobors, calumny of them, printed in the periodicals, bribery, flogging, prisons, deportation, the ruin of families. But the Dukhobors, on their side, have put forth nothing but their own religious instrument, meek reasonableness and long-suffering firmness, and say: "We must not obey men more than God, and no matter what they may do, we cannot and will not obey them."

They praise the Spanish and American heroes of that savage war, who, wishing to distinguish themselves in the eyes of men and to receive rewards and glory, have killed a very large number of men, or themselves have died in the process of slaying their neighbours.

But no one speaks or knows of these heroes of the war against war, who are not seen and heard by any one, who have died under rods or in stinking cells, or in oppressive exile, and still to their very last breath remain true to the good and to truth.

I know of dozens of these martyrs who have died, and hundreds who, scattered over the whole world, continue this martyrs' profession of the truth.

I know Drózhzhin, a peasant teacher, who was tortured to death in the disciplinary battalion; I know another, Izyumchénko, Drózhzhin's companion, who was kept awhile in the disciplinary battalion and then was sent away to the end of the world; I know Olkhóvik, a peasant, who refused to do military service, was for this sentenced to be sent to the disciplinary battalion, and on the boat converted his guard, Seredá. Sereda, who understood what Olkhóvik said about the sin of military service, came to the authorities and said, as the ancient martyrs said: "I do not want to be with the tormentors, join me to the martyrs," and they began to torture him, sent him to the disciplinary battalion, and then to Yakútsk Territory. I know dozens of Dukhobors, many of whom have died or grown blind, who none the less do not submit to the demands which are contrary to the law of God.

The other day I read a letter about a young Dukhobor who was sent by himself, without any companions, to a regiment stationed in Samarkand. Again the same demands on the part of the authorities, and the same simple, unswerving answers: "I cannot do what is contrary to my faith in God."—"We will torture you to death."—"That is your business. You do your business, and I will do mine."

And this twenty-year-old boy, cast by himself into a foreign country, amidst hostile people, strong, rich, cultured people, who direct all their forces to conquering him, does not succumb and does his great work.

They say: "These are useless sacrifices. These men will perish, but the structure of life will remain the same." Even thus, I think, people spoke of the uselessness of Christ's sacrifice and of the sacrifice of all the martyrs for the sake of truth. The people of our time, especially the scholars, have become so gross that they do not understand, and in their grossness cannot even understand, the significance and the influence of spiritual force. A charge of ten thousand pounds of dynamite sent into a crowd of living men,—that they understand, and in that they see strength; but an idea, truth, which has been realized, has been introduced into life to the point of martyrdom, has become accessible to millions,—that is according to their conception not force, because it does not boom, and you do not see broken bones and puddles of blood. Scholars (it is true, bad scholars) use all the power of their erudition to prove that humanity lives like a herd, which is guided only by economic conditions, and that reason is given to it only for amusement; but the governments know what it is that moves the world, and so unerringly, from a sense of self-preservation, look most zealously upon the manifestation of spiritual forces, on which depends their existence or their ruin. For this reason all the efforts of the Russian government have been directed upon making the Dukhobors harmless, upon isolating them and sending them abroad

But, in spite of all their efforts, the struggle of the Dukhobors has opened the eyes of millions.

I know hundreds of old and young military men who, thanks to the persecutions of the meek, industrious Dukhobors, have had misgivings as to the legality of their own activity; I know people who for the first time reflected upon life and the significance of Christianity, when they saw the life of these people or heard of the persecutions to which they have been subjected.

And the government, which rules over millions of people, knows this and feels that it has been struck at its very heart.

Such is the second war, which is being waged in our time, and such are its consequences. Its consequences are of importance, and not for the Russian government alone. Every government which is based on the army and on violence is struck in the same way by this weapon. Christ said, "I have conquered the world." He has really conquered the world, if people will only believe in the power of this weapon which is given to them.

This weapon is, for each man to follow his own reason and conscience.

This is so simple, so indubitable and obligatory for every single man. "You want to make me a participant in murder. You demand of me money for the preparation of the implements of murder, and you want me to become a participant in the organized gathering of murderers," says a rational man, who has not sold or dimmed his conscience. "But I confess the same law with you, in which not only murder, but even every hostility, has long ago been forbidden, and so I cannot obey you."

It is this means, which is so simple, that conquers the world.

Yásnaya Polyána, August 15, 1898.

LEO TOLSTOY

"Notes for Officers" (1901)

> *"It is impossible but that offenses*
> *will come, but woe unto him through*
> *whom they come"*
>
> LUKE *xvii. 1,2.*

Tolstoy, who as a young man served in the military in the Caucasus and wrote nonfictional and fictional accounts of the war there and in Crimea, is and was also known for his novel War and Peace. Here he addresses Russian military officers, who were compelling the "enslaved" soldiers to carry out "murder and the threat of murder" not only against foreign armies but against Russia's working class, their "own unarmed brothers who are by no means evil-doers, but peaceful, industrious men whose only desire is that they shall not be deprived of their earnings." He reminds the officers that they, unlike the soldiers, can resign: "If, however, you do not, it is only because you prefer to live and act against your conscience rather than lose certain worldly advantages."

IN ALL RUSSIAN barracks there hang, nailed to the wall, the so-called "Notes for Soldiers" composed by General Dragomiroff. These notes are a collection of stupidly braggart sentences intermixed with blasphemous citations from the Gospels, and written in an artificial barrack slang, which is, in reality, quite strange to every soldier. The Gospel citations are quoted in order to corroborate the statements that soldiers should kill and tear with their teeth the enemy: "If your bayonet breaks, strike with your fists; if your fists give way, bite with your teeth." The notes conclude with the statement that God is the soldier's General: "God is your General."

Nothing illustrates more convincingly than these notes that terrible degree of unenlightenment, servile submissiveness, and brutality which Russian men have attained to at present. Since this most horrible blasphemy appeared and was first hung up in all the

71

barracks (a considerable time ago), not one commander, nor priest—whom this distortion of the meaning of the Gospel texts would seem to concern directly—has expressed any condemnation of this obnoxious work and it continues to be published in millions of copies and to be read by millions of soldiers who accept this dreadful production as a guide to their conduct.

These notes revolted me long ago, and now, being afraid I may otherwise miss the opportunity of doing so before my death, I have now written an appeal to soldiers, in which I have endeavored to remind them that as men and Christians they have quite other duties toward God than those put forward in the notes. And a similar reminder is required, I think, not only by soldiers, but still more so by officers (by "officers" I mean all military authorities, from Subalterns to Generals), who enter the military service or continue in it, not by compulsion as privates do, but by their own free will. It was pardonable a hundred or fifty years ago, when war was regarded as an inevitable condition of the life of nations, when the men of the country with whom one was at war were regarded as barbarians, without religion, and evil-doers, and when it did not enter the mind of military men that they were required for the suppression and "pacification" of one's own people—it was pardonable then to put on a multi-colored uniform trimmed with gold braid and to saunter about with a clashing sword and jingling spurs, or to caracole in front of one's regiment, imagining oneself a hero, who, if he has not yet sacrificed his life for the defense of his fatherland, is nevertheless ready to do so. But at the present time, when frequent international communications, commercial, social, scientific, artistic, have so brought nations in touch with one another that any contemporary international war is like a dispute in a family, and breaks the most sacred human ties—when hundreds of peace societies and thousands of articles, not only in special but also in the ordinary newspapers, unceasingly demonstrate from every side the senselessness of militarism, and the possibility, even necessity, of abolishing war—at the present time, when, above all, the military are more and more often called out, not against foreign foes to repel invasions, or for the aggrandizement of the glory and power of their country, but against unarmed factory workmen or peasants—at the present time to caracole on one's little horse in one's little embroidered uniform and to advance dashingly at the head of one's company, is no longer a silly, pardonable piece of vanity as it was before, but something quite different.

In past times, in the days say of Nicholas I, (1825–1855), it entered into no one's head that troops are necessary chiefly to shoot at unarmed populaces. But at present troops are permanently stationed in every large town and manufacturing centre for the purpose of being ready to disperse gatherings of workmen; and seldom a month passes without soldiers being called out of their barracks with ball cartridges and hidden in secret places in readiness to shoot the populace down at any moment.

The use of troops against the people has become indeed not only customary—they are mobilized in advance to be in readiness for this very purpose; and the Governments do not conceal the fact that the distribution of recruits in the various regiments is intentionally conducted in such a way that the men are never drafted into a regiment stationed in the place from which they are drawn. This is done for the purpose of avoiding the possibility of soldiers having to shoot at their own relations.

The German Emperor, at every fresh call for recruits, has openly declared and still declares that soldiers who have been sworn in belong to him, body and soul; that they have only one foe—his foe; and that this foe are the Socialists (that is, workmen), whom the soldiers must, if he bids them, shoot down *(niederschiessen)*, even if they should be their own brothers or even parents.

In past times, moreover, if the troops were used against the people, those against whom they were used were, or at all events were supposed to be, evil-doers, ready to kill and ruin the peaceful inhabitants, and whom therefore it might be supposed to be necessary to destroy for the general good. But at present every one knows that those against whom troops are called out are for the most part peaceful, industrious men, who merely desire to profit unhindered by the fruits of their labors. So that the principal permanent function of the troops in our time no longer consists in an imaginary defense against irreligious and in general external foes, and not against internal foes in the persons of riotous evil-doers, but in killing one's own unarmed brothers, who are by no means evil-doers, but peaceful, industrious men whose only desire is that they shall not be deprived of their earnings. So that military service at the present time, when its chief object is, by murder and the threat of murder, to keep enslaved men in those unjust conditions in which they are placed, is not only not a noble but a positively dastardly undertaking. And therefore it is indispensable that officers who serve at the present time should consider whom they serve, and ask themselves whether what they are doing is good or evil.

I know that there are many officers, especially of the higher grades, who by various arguments on the themes of orthodoxy, autocracy, integrity of the State, eternal inevitableness of war, necessity of order, inconsistency of socialistic ravings, and so on, try to prove to themselves that their activity is rational and useful, and contains nothing immoral. But in the depths of their soul they themselves do not believe in what they say, and the more intelligent and the older they become the less they believe.

I remember how joyously I was struck by a friend and old comrade of mine, a very ambitious man, who had dedicated his whole life to military service, and had attained the highest honors and grades (General Aide-de-Camp and Major-General), when he told me that he had burnt his "Memoirs" of the wars in which he had participated because he had changed his view of the military activity, and now regarded every war as an evil deed, which should not be encouraged by participation, but, on the contrary, should be discredited in every way. Many officers think the same, although they do not say so while they serve. And indeed no thoughtful officer can think otherwise. Why, one has only to recall to mind what forms the occupation of all officers, from the lowest to the highest—to the Commandant of an Army Corps. From the beginning to the end of their service—I am alluding to officers in the active service—their activity, with the exception of the few and short periods when they go to war and are occupied with actual murder, consists in the attainment of two aims: in teaching soldiers the best methods of killing men, and in accustoming them to an obedience which enables them to do mechanically, without argument, everything their commander orders. In olden times it used to be said, "Flog two to death, and train one," and so they did. If at present the proportion of flogged to death is smaller, the principle nevertheless is the same. One cannot reduce men into that state, not of animals but of machines, in which they will commit the deed most repulsive to the nature of man and to the faith he professes, namely, murder, at the bidding of any commander—unless not only artful frauds but also the most cruel violence have been perpetrated on them. And so it is in practice.

Not long ago a great sensation was created in the French press by the disclosure by a journalist of those awful tortures to which soldiers in the Disciplinary Battalions are submitted on the Island of

Obrou, six hours' distance from Paris. The men punished have their hands and feet tied together behind their back and are then thrown to the ground; instruments are fixed on their thumbs while their hands are twisted behind their backs, and screwed up so that every movement produces a dreadful pain; they are hung with their legs upward; and so forth.

When we see trained animals accomplishing things contrary to nature: dogs walking on their forelegs, elephants rolling barrels, tigers playing with lions, and so on, we know that all this has been attained by the torments of hunger, whip, and red-hot iron. And when we see men in uniforms with rifles standing motionless, or performing all together with the same movement—running, jumping, shooting, shouting, and so on—in general, producing those fine reviews and manœuvers which emperors and kings so admire and show off one before the other, we know the same. One cannot cauterize out of a man all that is human and reduce him to the state of a machine without torturing him, and torturing not in a simple way but in the most refined, cruel way—at one and the same time torturing and deceiving him.

And all this is done by you officers. In this all your service consists, from the highest grade to the lowest, with the exception of those rare occasions when you participate in real war.

A youth transported from his family to the other end of the world comes to you, after having been taught that that deceptive oath forbidden by the Gospel which he has taken irretrievably binds him—as a cock when laid on the floor with a line drawn over its nose and along the floor thinks that it is bound by that line—he comes to you with complete submissiveness and the hope that you his elders, men more intelligent and learned than he, will teach him all that is good. And you, instead of freeing him from those superstitions which he has brought with him, inoculate him with new, most senseless, coarse, and pernicious superstitions: about the sanctity of the banner, the almost divine position of the Tsar, the duty of absolute obedience to the authorities. And when with the help of the methods for stultifying men which are elaborated in your organization you reduce him to a position worse than animal, to a position where he is ready to kill every one he is ordered to kill, even his unarmed brothers, you exhibit him with pride to your superiors, and receive in return their thanks and rewards. It is terrible to be a murderer oneself, but by cunning and cruel methods to reduce one's confiding brothers to this state is the most terrible crime of all. And this you accomplish, and in this consists the whole of your service.

It is therefore not astounding that amongst you more than amongst any other class everything which will stifle conscience flourishes: smoking, cards, drunkenness, depravity; and that suicides occur amongst you more frequently than anywhere else.

"It is impossible but that offenses will come, but woe unto him through whom they come."

You often say that you serve because if you did not the existing order would be destroyed and disturbances and every kind of calamities would occur.

But firstly, it is not true that you are concerned with the maintenance of the existing order: you are concerned only with your own advantages.

Secondly, even if your abstinence from military service did destroy the existing order, this would in no way prove that you should continue to do what is wrong, but only that the order which is being destroyed by your abstinence should be destroyed. Were establishments of the most useful kind—hospitals, schools, homes, to depend for their support on the profits from houses of ill-fame, no consideration of the good produced by these philanthropic establishments would retain in her position the woman who desired to free herself from her shameful trade.

"It is not my fault," the woman would say, "that you have founded your philanthropic institutions on vice. I no longer wish to live in vice. As to your institutions, they do not concern me." And so should every soldier say if the necessity of maintaining the existing order founded on his readiness to murder were put before him. "Organize the general order in a way that will not require murder," the soldier should say. "And then I shall not destroy it. I only do not wish to and cannot be a murderer."

Many of you say also: "I was educated thus. I am tied by my position, and cannot escape." But this also is not true.

You can always escape from your position. If, however, you do not, it is only because you prefer to live and act against your conscience rather than lose certain worldly advantages which your dishonest service affords. Only forget that you are an officer and recall to mind that you are a man, and the way of escape from your position will immediately disclose itself to you. This way of escape in its best and most honest form would consist in your calling together the men of whom you are in command, stepping in front, and asking their pardon for all the evil you have done them by deception—and then cease to serve in the army. Such an action seems very bold, demanding great courage, whereas in reality much less courage is required for such an action than to storm a fortification or to challenge a man to a duel for an insult to the uniform—which you as a soldier are always ready to do, and do.

But even without being capable of acting thus you can always, if you have understood the criminality of military service, leave it and give preference to any other activity though less advantageous.

But if you cannot do even this, then the solution for you of the question whether you will continue to serve or not will be postponed to that time—and this will soon appear for each one of you—when you will stand face to face with an unarmed crowd of peasants or factory workers, and be ordered to shoot at them. And then, if anything human remains in you, you will have to refuse to obey, and, as a result, to leave the service.

I know that there are still many officers, from the highest to the lowest ranks, who are so unenlightened or hypnotized that they do not see the necessity of either the one, the other, or the third solution, and quietly continue to serve even in the present conditions, ready to shoot at their brothers and even priding themselves upon this; but happily public opinion punishes such people with more and more repulsion and disapproval, and their number continually becomes smaller and smaller.

So that in our time, when the fratricidal function of the army has become evident, officers not only can no longer continue in the ancient traditions of military self-complacent bravado—they cannot continue the criminal work of teaching murder to simple men confiding in them, and themselves to prepare for participation in murdering unarmed populaces, without the consciousness of their human degradation and shame.

It is this which should be understood and remembered by every thinking and conscientious officer of our time.

LEO TOLSTOY

"I Cannot Be Silent" (1908)

As an activist and the greatest author of his time, Tolstoy was one of the most famous people in the world when he wrote and published internationally (it was forbidden to be published in Russia but was anyway) "I Cannot Be Silent" (published on one full sheet in the Sunday magazine section of The New York Times on July 19, 1908). Tolstoy was never so publicly provocative or unhappy as he was in this essay. It draws out not just his customary brilliant coherence and clarity but his despair over what the Russian government had come to by its justifying its use of capital punishment. His words did not after all immediately "break cement"; they did however lay out paths for his future countrymen Aleksandr Solzhenitsyn's and Nadezhda Tolokonnikova's own civilly disobedient protest statements: "an exposure of these people who do not see the full criminality of their actions is necessary for them as well as for the multitude which, influenced by the external honour and laudation accorded to these people, approves their terrible deeds and even tries to imitate them. [...] I hope my exposure of those men will in one way or other evoke the expulsion I desire from the set in which I am now living, and in which I cannot but feel myself a participant in the crimes committed around me." The government, rather than expelling Tolstoy from Russia and exposing itself to the world's further scorn, ignored him until his death two years later.

THE FREQUENCY OF Executions in Russia Provokes a Denunciation of Government That Spares Neither Czar, Church, Nor Duma.
(No Rights Reserved)
"People Flatter You Because at Heart They Despise and Hate You—And You Know It and Are Afraid of Men"—to the Czar.

"Seven death sentences: two in St. Petersburg, one in Moscow, two in Penza, and two in Riga. Four executions: two in Kherson, one in Vilna, one in Odessa."

This, daily repeated in every newspaper and continued, not for weeks, not months, not for one year, but for years! And this in

78

Russia, that same Russia where the people regard every criminal as a man to be pitied, and where till quite recently capital punishment was not recognized by law! I remember how proud I used to be of that, when talking to Western Europeans; but now for a second and even a third year, we have executions, executions, executions, unceasingly!

I take up today's paper.

To-day, the 9th of May, it is something awful. The paper contains these few words: "To-day in Kherson on the Strelbitsky Field twenty* peasants were hanged for an attack made with intent to rob, on a landed proprietor's estate in the Elizabetgrad district."

Twelve of those by whose labor we live, the very men whom we have depraved and are still depraving by every means in our power—from the poison of vodka to the terrible falsehood of a creed we do not ourselves believe in, but impose on them with all our sight—twelve of these men, strangled with cords by those whom they feed and clothe and house, and who have depraved and still continue to deprave them. Twelve husbands, fathers, sons, from among those on whose kindness, industry, and simplicity alone rests the whole of Russian life, were seized, imprisoned, and shackled. Then their hands were tied behind their backs, lest they should seize the ropes by which they would be hanged, and they were led to the gallows. Several peasants similar to those who are about to be hanged, but armed, dressed in clean soldiers' uniforms, with good boots on their feet and with guns in their hands, accompany the condemned men. Beside them walks a long-haired man, wearing a stole and vestments of gold or silver cloth, and bearing a cross. The procession stops. The manager of the whole business says something; the secretary reads a paper; and when the paper has been read, the long-haired man, addressing those whom other people are about to strangle with cords, says something about God and Christ.

---

* The papers have since contradicted the statement that twenty peasants were hanged. I can only be glad of the mistake, glad not only that eight men less have been strangled than was stated at first, but glad also that the awful figures moved me to express in these pages a feeling that has long tormented me. Therefore, merely substituting the word twelve for the word twenty, I leave all the rest unchanged, since what I said refers not only to the twelve who were hanged, but to all the thousands who have likely been crushed and killed.

Immediately after these words, the hangman (there are several, for one man could not manage so complicated a business) dissolves some soap, and having soaped the loops in the cords that they may tighten better, seize the shackled men, put shrouds on them, lead them to a scaffold, and place the well-soaped nooses around their necks.

Revolting Executions Planned by Learned Men of Upper Class.

And then, one after another, living men are pushed off the benches which are drawn from under their feet, and by their own weight suddenly tighten the nooses around their necks, and are painfully strangled. Men, alive a minute before, become corpses dangling from a rope; at first slowly swinging. and then resting motionless.

All this is carefully arranged and planned by learned and enlightened people of the upper class. They arrange to do these things secretly at day break, so that no one should see them done, and they arrange that the responsibility for these iniquities shall be so subdivided among those who commit them that each may think and say it is not he who is responsible for them. They arrange to seek out the most depraved and unfortunate of men, and while obliging them to do this business, planned and approved by us, still keep up an appearance of abhorring those who do it. Even such a subtle device is planned as this: Sentences are pronounced by a military tribunal, yet it is not the military but civilians who have to be present at the execution. And the business is performed by unhappy, deluded, perverted, and despised men who have nothing left them but to soap the cords well that they may grip the necks without fail, then to get well drunk on poison sold them by these same enlightened upper-class people, in order more quickly and fully to forget their souls and their quality as men. A doctor makes his round of the bodies, feels them, and reports to those in authority that the business has been done properly; all twelve are certainly dead. And those in authority depart to their ordinary occupations with the consciousness of a necessary though painful task performed. The bodies, now grown cold, are taken down and buried.

The thing is awful!

And this is not done once, and not to these twelve unhappy, misguided men from among the best class of the Russian people only, but it is done unceasingly for years, to hundreds and thousands of similar misguided men, misguided by the very people who do these awful things to them.

And not this kind of dreadful thing alone is being done, but on the same plea and with the same cold-blooded cruelty all sorts of other tortures and violence are being perpetrated in prisons, fortresses, and convlot settlements.

And while this goes on for years all over Russia, the chief culprits of these acts—those by whose order these things are done, those who could put a stop to them—fully convinced that such deeds are useful and even absolutely necessary, either devise methods and make up speeches how to prevent the Finns from living as they want to live, and how to compel them to live as certain Russian personages wish them to live; or else publish orders to the effect that "In Hussar regiments the cuffs and collars of the men's jackets are to be of the color of the latter, while the pelisses of those entitled to wear them are not to have braid around the cuffs over the fur."

This is awful!

II.

What is most dreadful in the whole matter is that all this inhuman violence and killing, besides the direct evil done to the victims and their families, brings a yet more enormous evil on the whole people by spreading depravity—as fire spreads amid dry straw—among every class of Russians. This depravity grows with special rapidity among the simple working folk, because all these iniquities— exceeding as they do a hundredfold all that has been done by thieves, robbers, and by all the revolutionaries put together—are done as though they were something necessary, good, and unavoidable, and are not merely excused but supported by different institutions inseparably connected in the people's minds with Jus- tice, and even with sanctity—namely, the Senate, the Synod, the Duma, the Church, and the Czar.

And this depravity spreads with remarkable rapidity.

A short time ago there were not two executioners to be found in all Russia. In the eighties there was only one. I remember how joyfully Vladimir Solovyof told me at that time that no second executioner could be found in all Russia, and so the one was taken from place to place. Not so now!

A small shopkeeper in Moscow whose affairs were in a bad way having offered his services to perform the murders arranged by Government, and receiving a hundred rubles (£10) for each person hanged soon mended his affairs so well that he no longer required this additional business, and is now carrying on his former trade.

In Orel last month, as everywhere else, an executioner was wanted, and at once a man was found who agreed with the organizers of Governmental murders to do the business for 50 rubles per head. But the volunteer hangman, after making this agreement, heard that more was paid in other towns, and at the time of the execution, having put the shroud sack on the victim, instead of leading him to the scaffold, stopped, and approaching the Superintendent, said: "You must add another 25 rubles, your Excellency, or I won't do it!" He got the increase and he did the job.

Taking Men's Lives Subject to Barter and Sale

The next time five were to be hanged. The day before the execution a stranger came to see the organizer of Governmental murders on a private matter. The organizer went out to him, and the stranger said:

"T'other day So-and-so charged you 75 rubles per man. To-day I hear five are to be done. Let me have the whole job and I'll do it at 15 rubles a head, and you may be sure it shall be done properly."

I do not know whether the offer was accepted or not; but I know it was made.

That is how the crimes committed by the Government act on the worst, the least moral, of the people; and these terrible deeds must also have an influence on the majority of men of average morality. Continually hearing and reading about the most terrible, inhuman brutality committed by the authorities—that is by persons whom the people are accustomed to honor as the best of men—the majority of average people, especially the young, preoccupied with their own affairs, instead of realizing that those who do such horrid deeds are unworthy of honor, involuntarily come to the opposite conclusion. and argue that if men generally honored do things that seem to us horrible, probably these things are not as horrible as we suppose.

Of executions, hangings, murders, and bombs people now write and speak as they used to speak about the weather. Children play at hangings. Lads from the high schools, who are almost children, go out on expropriating expeditions, ready to kill, just as they used to go out hunting. To kill off the large landed proprietors in order to seize their estates appears now to many people to be the very best solution of the land question.

In general, thanks to the activity of the Government, which has allowed killing as a means of obtaining its ends, all crimes—robbery, theft, lies, tortures, and murder—are now considered by miserable people who have been perverted by the Government to be most natural deeds, proper to a man.

Yes: Awful as are the deeds themselves, the moral, spiritual unseen evil they produce is incomparably more terrible.

III.

You say you commit all these horrors to restore peace and order.

You restore peace and order. By what means do you restore them? By the fact that you, representatives of a Christian authority, leaders and teachers approved and encouraged by the servants of the Church, destroy the last vestige of faith and morality in men by committing the greatest crimes—lies, perfidy, torture of all sorts, and the last, most awful of crimes, the one most abhorrent to every human heart not utterly depraved—not just a murder, a single murder, but murders innumerable, which you think to justify by stupid references to such and such statutes written by yourselves, in those stupid and lying books of yours which you blasphemously call The Laws.

Private Property in Land a Cause of Trouble

You say that this is the only means of pacifying the people and quelling the revolution; but that is evidently false! It is plain that you cannot pacify the people unless you satisfy the demand of most elementary justice advanced by Russia's whole agricultural population, namely, the demand for the abolition of private property in land, and refrain from confirming it and in various ways irritating the peasants, as well as those unbalanced and envenomed people who have begun a violent strggle with you. You cannot pacify people by tormenting them and worrying, exiling, imprisoning, and hanging women and children! However hard you may try to stifle in yourselves the reason and love natural to human beings, you still have them within you, and need only come to your senses and think in order to see that by acting as you do—that is by taking part in such terrible crimes—you not only fail to cure the disease, but, by driving it inward, make it worse.

This is only too evident.

The cause of what is happening does not lie in physical events, but depends entirely on the spiritual mood of the people, which has changed, and which no efforts can bring back to its former condition, just as no efforts can turn a grown-up man into a child again. Social irritation or tranquillity cannot depend on whether Peter is alive or hanged, or on whether John lives in Tambof or in penal servitude at Nertchinsk. Social irritation or tranquillity must depend not on how Peter or John alone but how the great majority of the nation regard their position, and on the attitude of this majority to the Government, to landed property, to the religion taught them, and on what this majority consider to be good or bad. The power of events by no means lies in the material conditions of life, but in the spiritual condition of the people. Though you were even to kill and torture a whole tenth of the Russian nation, the spiritual condition of the rest would not become such as you desire.

So that all you are now doing with all your searchings, spyings, eviling, prisons, penal settlements, and gallows does not bring the people to the state you desire, but on the contrary increases the irritation and destroys all possibility of pacification.

"But what is to be done?" you say. "What is to be done? How are the iniquities that are now perpetrated to be stopped?"

The answer is very simple: "Cease to do what you are doing."

Even if no one knew what ought to be done to pacify "the people"—the whole people—(many people know very well that what is most wanted for the pacifying of the Russian people is the freeing of the land from private ownership, just as fifty years ago what was wanted was to free the peasants from serfdom)—if no one knew this it would still be evident that to pacify the people one ought not to do what but increases its irritation. Yet that is just what you are doing.

Real Motive for Executions a Purely Selfish One

What you are doing you do not for the people, but for yourselves to retain the position you occupy, a position you erroneously consider advantageous, but which is really a most pitiful and abominable one. So do not say that you do it for the people; that is not true! All the abominations you do are done for yourselves, for your own covetous, ambitious, vain, vindictive, personal ends, in order to continue a little longer in the depravity in which you live and which seems to you desirable.

However much you may declare that all you do is done for the good of the people, men are beginning more and more to understand you, and ever more and more to despise you, and to regard your measures of restraint and suppression not as you wish them to be regarded, as the action of some kind of higher collective being, the Government—but as the personal evil deeds of separate evil self-seekers.

IV

Again, you say: "Not we, but the revolutionaries, began all this; and the terrible crimes of the revolutionaries can only be suppressed by firm measures (so you call your crimes) on the part of the Government."

You say the atrocities committed by the revolutionaries are terrible.

I do not dispute it, but add that besides being terrible they are also stupid, and—like your own actions—hit beside the mark. Yet, however terrible and stupid may be their actions, all those bombs and tunnelings, and those revolting murders and thefts of money—still, all these deeds do not come anywhere near the criminality and stupidity of the deeds you commit.

They are doing just the same as you, and for the same motives. They are in the same (I should say "comical," were its consequences not so awful) delusion, that men having formed for themselves a plan of what in their opinion is the desirable and proper arrangement of society, have the right and possibility of arranging other people's lives according to that plan. The delusion is the same. These methods are violence of all kinds—including taking life. And I the excuse is, that an evil deed committed for the benefit of many ceases to be immoral; and that, therefore, without offending against the moral law, one may lie, rob, and kill whenever this leads to the realization of that proposed good condition for the many which we imagine that we know and can foresee, and which we wish to establish.

You, Government men, call the acts of the revolutionaries "atrocities" and "great crimes," but they have done and are doing nothing that you have not done, and done to an incomparably greater extent. They only do what you do: You keep spies, deceive, and spread printed lies, and so do they. You take people's property by all sorts of violent means and use it as you consider best, and they do the same. You execute those whom you think dangerous, and so do they.

So that while employing the same immoral means as they do for the attainment of your aim, you certainly cannot blame the revolutionaries. All you can adduce for your own justification, they can equally adduce for theirs; not to mention that you do much evil they do not commit, such as squandering the wealth of the nation, preparing for war, making war, and subduing and oppressing foreign nationalities, and much else.

You say you have the traditions of the past to guard, and the actions of the great men of the past as examples. They, too, have their traditions also arising from the past, even before the French Revolution; and as to great men, models to copy martyrs that perished for truth and freedom—they have no fewer of these than you.

So that, if there is any difference between you it is only that you wish everything to remain as it has been and is, while they wish for a change. And in thinking that everything cannot always remain as it used to be, they would be more right than you, had they not adopted from you that curious, destructive delusion, that one set of men can know a form of life suitable for all men in the future, and that this form can be established by force. For the rest, they only do what you do, using the same means. They are altogether your disciples; they have, as the saying is, picked up all your little dodges; they are not only your disciples, they are your products, your children. If you did not exist, neither would they; so that when you try to suppress them by force, you behave like a man who presses with his whole weight against a door that opens toward him.

Revolutionary Not So Vicious as Legal Violence

If there be any difference between you and them, it is certainly not in your, but in their, favor. The mitigating circumstances on their side are, first, that their crimes are committed under conditions of greater personal danger than you are exposed to; and risks and dangers excuse much in the eyes of impressionable youth. Secondly, that the immense majority of them are quite young people, to whom it is natural to go astray, while you are for the most part men of mature age; old men to whom reasonable calmness and leniency toward the deluded should be natural. Thirdly a mitigating circumstance in their favor is that however odious their murders may be, they are still not so coldly, systematically cruel as your Schlusselburgs, transportations, gallows, and shootings. The fourth mitigating circumstance for the revolutionaries is, that they all quite categorically repudiate all religious teaching, and consider that the end justifies the means, and therefore they act quite consistently when they kill one or more men for the sake of the imaginary welfare of the many; whereas you, Government men—from the lowest hangmen to the highest of those who command them—you all support religion and Christianity, which is altogether incompatible with the deeds you commit.

And it is you elderly men, leaders of other men, professing Christianity, it is you who say, like children who have been fighting, "We didn't begin; they did"! And that is the best you can say, you who have taken on yourselves the role of rulers of the people. And what sort of men are you? Men who acknowledge as God, one who most definitely forbade not only judgment and punishment, but even the condemnation of one's brother; one who in clearest terms repudiated all punishment and affirmed the necessity of continual forgiveness however often a crime may be repeated; one who commanded us to turn the other cheek to the smiter and not to return evil for evil; one who, in the story of the woman sentenced to be stoned, showed so simply and clearly the impossibility of judgment and punishment between man and man. And you, acknowledging that teacher to be God, can find nothing better to say in your defense than that "They began, they kill; so let us kill them"!

V

An artist of my acquaintance thought of painting a picture, "The Execution," and he wanted a model for the executioner. He heard that the duty of executioner in Moscow was at that time performed by a watchman. The artist went to the watchman's house. It was Easter-time. The family were sitting in their best clothes at the tea table, but the master of the house was not there. It turned out afterward that on catching sight of a stranger he had hidden himself. His wife also seemed abashed, and said that her husband was not at home; but his little girl betrayed him by saying "Daddy's in the garret." She did not know that her father was aware that he was doing evil, and could not help therefore being afraid of anybody. The artist explained to the wife that he wanted her husband as a model to paint, because his face suited the picture he had planned, (of course the artist did not say what the picture was for which he wanted the watchman's face.) Having got into conversation with the wife, the artist, to conciliate her, offered to take her little son as a pupil. This offer evidently tempted the woman. She went out and after a time the husband entered, looking askance, morose, restless, and frightened. He long tried to get the artist to say why and for what he required just him. When the artist told him he had met him in the street and his face seemed suitable to the projected picture, the watchman asked, Where he had met him? at what time? In what clothes? And, evidently fearing and suspecting something evil, would not come to terms.

The Czar and All Officials Are Participators

Yes. this executioner at first hand knows that he is an executioner, and that he does wrong and is therefore hated, and he is afraid of men, and I think this consciousness and this fear before men atone for at least a part of his guilt. But you all, from the Secretary of the court to the Premier and the Czar—you indirect participators in the iniquities perpetrated every day—do not seem to feel your guilt, nor the shame your participation in these horrors would evoke. It is true that like the executioner, you fear men, and fear the more the greater your responsibility for the crimes; the Public Prosecutor more than the Secretary; the President of the Court more than the Public Prosecutor; the General Governor more than the President; the President of the Council of Ministers more still, and the Czar most of all. You are all afraid; but unlike that executioner you are afraid not because you know you are doing evil, but because you think other people do evil.

Therefore I think that low as that unfortunate watchman has fallen, he stands morally immeasurably higher than you, participators and part authors of these awful crimes; you who condemn others instead of yourselves, and carry your heads so high.

VI

I know that men are but human, that we all are weak that we all err, and that one cannot judge another. I have long struggled against the feeling that was and is aroused in me by those responsible for these awful crimes, and aroused the more the higher they stand on the social ladder. But I neither can nor will struggle against that feeling any longer.

I cannot and will not; first, because an exposure of these people who do not see the full criminality of their actions is necessary for them as well as for the multitude that, influenced by the external honor and laudation accorded to these persons, approve their terrible deeds and even try to imitate them. Secondly, I cannot and will not struggle any longer, because (I frankly confess it) I hope my exposure of those men will one way or other, evoke the expulsion I desire from the set in which I am now living, and in which I cannot but feel myself to be a participator in the crimes committed around me.

Everything now being done in Russia is done in the name of the general welfare, in the name of the protection and tranquillity of the inhabitants of Russia. And if this be so, then it is also all done for me, who lives in Russia. For me, therefore, exists the destitution of the people, deprived of the first, most natural right of man— the right to use the land on which he is born; for me the half million men torn away from wholesome peasant life, and dressed in uniforms and taught to kill; for me that false so-called priesthood, whose chief duty it is to pervert and conceal true Christianity; for me all these transportations of men from place to place; for me these hundreds of thousands of hungry workmen wandering about Russia; for me these hundreds of thousands of unfortunates dying of typhus and scurvy in the fortresses and prisons which do not suffice for such a multitude; for me the mothers, wives, and fathers of the exiles, the prisoners, and those who are hung, are suffering; for me are these spies and this bribery; for me the interment of these dozens and hundreds of men who have been shot; for me the horrible work goes on of these hangmen, at first enlisted with difficulty, but now no longer so loathing their work; for me exist these gallows, with well-soaped cords, from which hang women, children, and peasants; for me exists this terrible embitterment of man against his fellow-man.

Strange as is the statement that all this is done for me, and that I am a participator in these terrible deeds, I cannot but feel that there is an indubitable interdependence between my spacious room, my dinner, my clothing, my leisure, and these terrible crimes committed to get rid of those who would like to take from me what I use. And though I know that these homeless, embittered, depraved people—who but for the Government's threats would deprive me of all I am using—are produces of that same Government's actions, still I cannot help feeling that at present my peace really is dependent on all the horrors that are now being perpetrated by the Government.

And being conscious of this I can no longer endure it, but must free myself from this intolerable position!

It is impossible to live so! I, at any rate, cannot and will not live so. That is why I write this, and will circulate it by all means in my power, both in Russia and abroad; that one of two things may happen: either that these inhuman deeds may be stopped or that my connection with them may be snapped and I put in prison where I may be clearly conscious that these horrors are not committed on my behalf; or still better, (so good that I dare not even dream of such happiness) they may put on me, as on those twenty or twelve peasants, a shroud and a cap and may push me also off a bench, so that by my own weight I may tighten the well-soaped noose around my old throat.

To attain one of these two aims, I address myself to all the participators in these terrible deeds, beginning with those who put on their brother men and women and children those caps and nooses—from the prison warders up to you, chief organizers and authorizers of these terrible crimes.

Brother men! Come to your senses! Stop and think! Consider what you are doing! Remember who you are!

Importance of Humanity Greater than Officialdom

Before being hangmen, Generals, Public Prosecutors, Judges, Premier, or Czar—are you not men? To-day allowed a peep into God's world, to-morrow ceasing to be. (You hangmen of all grades in particular, who have evoked and are evoking special hatred, should remember this.) Is it possible that you, who have had this short glimpse of God's world, (for even if you be not murdered death is always close behind us all.) is it possible that in your lucid moments you do not see that your vocation in life cannot be to torment and kill men; yourselves trembling with fear of being killed, lying to yourselves, to others, and to God, assuring yourselves and others that by participating in these things you are doing an important and grand work for the welfare of millions? Is it possible that—when not intoxicated by your surroundings, by flattery, and by the customary sophistries—you do not each one of you know that all this is mere talk, only invented that while doing most evil deeds you may still consider yourself a good man? You cannot but know that you, like each of us, have but one real duty, which includes all others: the duty of living the short space granted us in accord with the Will that sent you into this world, and of leaving it in accord with that Will. And that Will desires only one thing: love from man to man.

But what are you doing? To what are you devoting your spiritual strength? Whom do you love? Who loves you? Your wife? Your child? But that is not love. The love of wife and children is not human love. Animals love in that way even more strongly. Human love is the love of man for man—for every man as a son of God, and therefore a brother.

Whom do you love in that way? No one. Who loves you in that way ? No one.

You are feared as the hangman or a wild animal is feared. People flatter you because at heart they despise and hate you—and how they do hate you! And you know it, and are afraid of men.

Yes, consider it, all of you from the highest to the lowest accomplices in murder; consider who you are, and cease to do what you are doing. Cease not for your own sakes, not for the sake of your own personality, not for the sake of men, not that you may cease to be blamed but for your soul's sake and for the God who lives within you!

June 13, 1908.

MAHATMA GANDHI

The Theory and Practice of Satyagraha (1914)

Born in western India in 1869, Mohandas Karamchand Gandhi ("Mahatma," meaning "great-souled," was a title bestowed on him later by his followers), was the twentieth century's most influential hero of peaceful revolution, inspiring, among others, Martin Luther King, Jr., and Burma's Aung San Suu Kyi. Gandhi earned his law degree in London in 1891 and practiced in South Africa for twenty-one years before returning to India in 1914 as an advocate for satyagraha (usually translated as "passive resistance" but literally "truth-force" or "soul-force"). The British authorities repeatedly jailed Gandhi for his teachings, despite their basis in the peace-inspired texts of the major religions. "This Satyagraha did not fail me in South Africa, Kheda, or Champaran and in a host of other cases I could mention," said Gandhi in his Presidential Address to the Indian National Congress in December of 1924. "It excludes all violence or hate. Therefore, I cannot and will not hate Englishmen. Nor will I bear their yoke. I must fight unto death the unholy attempt to impose British methods and British institutions on India. But I combat the attempt with non-violence. I have repeatedly stated that Satyagraha never fails and that one perfect Satyagrahi is enough to vindicate Truth."[1] Gandhi led the nationalist movement in India that resulted in the country's independence in August 1947; five months later a Hindu nationalist fanatic assassinated him.

"The Theory of Practice of Satyagraha" serves as a description of the difficulties and trials of adhering to nonresistance principles. While Tolstoy and Thoreau seemed to see the immediate change that could come about through following one's conscience, Gandhi believed in the necessity of dedicated training: "It is impossible for those who consider themselves to be weak to apply this force. Only those who realize that there is something in man which is superior to the brute nature in him and that the latter always yields to it, can effectively be Satyagrahis."

---

[1] M. K. Gandhi. "My Faith." In *Non-Violent Resistance (Satyagraha)*. Mineola, New York: Dover. 2001. 176.

[The following is taken from an article by Gandhiji contributed to the Golden Number of *Indian Opinion* which was issued in 1914 as a souvenir of the eight years' Satyagraha in South Africa:]

CARRIED OUT TO its utmost limit, Satyagraha is independent of pecuniary or other material assistance; certainly, even in its elementary form, of physical force or violence. Indeed, violence is the negation of this great spiritual force, which can only be cultivated or wielded by those who will entirely eschew violence. It is a force that may be used by individuals as well as by communities. It may be used as well in political as in domestic affairs. Its universal applicability is a demonstration of its permanence and invincibility. It can be used alike by men, women and children. It is totally untrue to say that it is a force to be used only by the weak so long as they are not capable of meeting violence by violence. This superstition arises from the incompleteness of the English expression, *passive resistance*. It is impossible for those who consider themselves to be weak to apply this force. Only those who realize that there is something in man which is superior to the brute nature in him and that the latter always yields to it, can effectively be Satyagrahis. This force is to violence, and, therefore, to all tyranny, all injustice, what light is to darkness. In politics, its use is based upon the immutable maxim, that government of the people is possible only so long as they consent either consciously or unconsciously to be governed. We did not want to be governed by the Asiatic Act of 1907 of the Transvaal, and it had to go before this mighty force. Two courses were open to us: to use violence when we were called upon to submit to the Act, or to suffer the penalties prescribed under the Act, and thus to draw out and exhibit the force of the soul within us for a period long enough to appeal to the sympathetic chord in the governors or the law-makers. We have taken long to achieve what we set about striving for. That was because our Satyagraha was not of the most complete type. All Satyagrahis do not understand the full value of the force, nor have we men who always from conviction refrain from violence. The use of this force requires the adoption of poverty, in the sense that we must be indifferent whether we have the wherewithal to feed or clothe ourselves. During the past struggle, all Satyagrahis, if any at all, were not prepared to go that length. Some again were only Satyagrahis so called. They came without any conviction, often with mixed motives, less often with impure motives. Some even, whilst engaged in the struggle, would gladly have resorted to violence but for most vigilant supervision. Thus it was that the struggle became prolonged; for the exercise of the purest soul-force, in its perfect form, brings about instantaneous relief. For this exercise, prolonged training of the individual soul is an absolute necessity, so that a perfect Satyagrahi has to be almost, if not entirely, a perfect man. We cannot all suddenly become such men, but if my proposition is correct—as I know it to be correct—the greater the spirit of Satyagraha in us, the better men will we become. Its use, therefore, is, I think, indisputable, and it is a force, which, if it became universal, would revolutionize social ideals and do away with despotisms and the ever-growing militarism under which the nations of the West are groaning and are being almost crushed to death, and which fairly promises to overwhelm even the nations of the East. If the past struggle has produced even a few Indians who would dedicate themselves to the task of becoming Satyagrahis as nearly perfect as possible, they would not only have served themselves in the truest sense of the term, they would also have served humanity at large. Thus viewed, Satyagraha is the noblest and best education. It should come, not after the ordinary education in letters, of children, but it should precede it. It will not be denied, that a child, before it begins to write its alphabet and to gain worldly knowledge, should know what the soul is, what truth is, what love is, what powers are latent in the soul. It should be an essential of real education that a child should learn, that in the struggle of life, it can easily conquer hate by love, untruth by truth, violence by self-suffering.

MAHATMA GANDHI

Ahmedabad (1919)

("For me life would not be worth living if Ahmedabad
continues to countenance violence in the name of truth")
Ahmedabad, India
April 14, 1919

On April 13, 1919, British troops shot and killed 400 nonviolent demonstrators who had gathered to call for Indian independence from Great Britain. After an outbreak of riots, Gandhi made this speech the next day from his ashram to the citizens of Ahmedabad.

BROTHERS,—I MEAN to address myself mainly to you. Brothers, the events that have happened in course of the last few days have been most disgraceful to Ahmedabad, and as all these things have happened in my name, I am ashamed of them, and those who have been responsible for them have thereby not honoured me but disgraced me. A rapier run through my body could hardly have pained me more. I have said times without number that Satyagraha admits of no violence, no pillage, no incendiarism; and still in the name of Satyagraha we burnt down buildings, forcibly captured weapons, extorted money, stopped trains, cut off telegraph wires, killed innocent people and plundered shops and private houses. If deeds such as these could save me from the prison house or the scaffold I should not like to be so saved. I do wish to say in all earnestness that violence has not secured my discharge. A most brutal rumour was set afloat that Anasuya Bai was arrested. The crowds were infuriated all the more, and disturbance increased. You have thereby disgraced Anasuya Bai and under the cloak of her arrest heinous deeds have been done.

These deeds have not benefited the people in any way. They have done nothing but harm. The buildings burnt down were

95

public property and they will naturally be rebuilt at our expense. The loss due to the shops remaining closed is also our loss. The terrorism prevailing in the city due to Martial Law is also the result of this violence. It has been said that many innocent lives have been lost as a result of the operation of Martial Law. If this is a fact then for that too the deeds described above are responsible. It will thus be seen that the events that have happened have done nothing but harm to us. Moreover they have most seriously damaged the Satyagraha movement. Had an entirely peaceful agitation followed my arrest, the Rowlatt Act would have been out or on the point of being out of the Statute Book today. It should not be a matter for surprise if the withdrawal of the Act is now delayed. When I was released on Friday my plan was to start for Delhi again on Saturday to seek rearrest, and that would have been an accession of strength to the movement. Now, instead of going to Delhi, it remains to me to offer Satyagraha against our own people, and as it is my determination to offer Satyagraha even unto death for secur- ing the withdrawal of the Rowlatt legislation, I think the occasion has arrived when I should offer Satyagraha against ourselves for the violence that has occurred. And I shall do so at the sacrifice of my body, so long as we do not keep perfect peace and cease from vio- lence to person and property. How can I seek imprisonment unless I have absolute confidence that we shall no longer be guilty of such errors? Those desirous of joining the Satyagraha movement or of helping it must entirely abstain from violence. They may not resort to violence even on my being rearrested or on some such events happening. Englishmen and women have been compelled to leave their homes and confine themselves to places of protection in Shahi Bag, because their trust in our harmlessness has received a rude shock. A little thinking should convince us that this is a matter of humiliation for us all. The sooner this state of things stops the bet- ter for us. They are our brethren and it is our duty to inspire them with the belief that their persons are as sacred to us as our own and this is what we call *Abhaydan*, the first requisite of true religion. Satyagraha without this is *Duxagraha*.

There are two distinct duties now before us. One is that we should firmly resolve upon refraining from all violence, and the other is that we should repent and do penance for our sins. So long as we don't repent and do not realise our errors and make an open confession of them, we shall not truly change our course. The first step is that those of us who have captured weapons should surrender them. To show that we are really penitent we will contribute each of us not less than eight annas towards helping the families of those who have been killed by our acts. Though no amount of money contribution can altogether undo the results of the furious deeds of the past few days, our contribution will be a slight token of our repentence. I hope and pray that no one will evade this contribution on the plea that he has had no part in those wicked acts. For if such as those who were no party to these deeds had all courageously and bravely gone forward to put down the lawlessness, the mob would have been checked in their career and would have immediately realised the wickedness of their doings. I venture to say that if instead of giving money to the mob out of fear we had rushed out to protect buildings and to save the innocent without fear of death we could have succeeded in so doing. Unless we have this sort of courage, mischief-makers will always try to intimidate us into participating in their misdeeds. Fear of death makes us devoid both of valour and religion. For want of valour is want of religious faith. And having done little to stop the violence we have been all participators in the sins that have been committed. And we ought, therefore, to contribute our mite as a mark of our repentence. Each group can collect its own contributions and send them on to me through its collectors. I would also advise, if it is possible for you, to observe a twenty-four hours fast in slight expiation of these sins. This fast should be observed in private and there is no need for crowds to go to the bathing ghats.

I have thus far drawn attention to what appears to be your duty. I must now consider my own. My responsibility is a million times greater than yours. I have placed Satyagraha before people for their acceptance, and I have lived in your midst for four years. I have also given some contribution to the special service of Ahmedabad. Its citizens are not quite unfamiliar with my views.

It is alleged that I have without proper consideration persuaded thousands to join the movement. That allegation is, I admit, true to a certain extent, but to a certain extent only. It is open to any body to say that but for the Satyagraha campaign there would not have been this violence. For this I have already done a penance, to my mind an unendurable one, namely, that I have had to postpone my visit to Delhi to seek rearrest and I have also been obliged to suggest a temporary restriction of Satyagraha to a limited field. This has been more painful to me than a wound but this penance is not enough, and I have therefore decided to fast for three days, *i.e.,*

72 hours. I hope my fast will pain no one. I believe a seventy-two hours fast is easier for me than a twenty-four hours' fast for you. And I have imposed on me a discipline which I can bear. If you really feel pity for the suffering that will be caused to me, I request that that pity should always restrain you from ever again being party to the criminal acts of which I have complained. Take it from me that we are not going to win Swarajya or benefit our country in the least by violence and terrorism. I am of opinion that if we have to wade through violence to obtain Swarajya and if a redress of grievances were to be only possible by means of ill will for and slaughter of English men I for one would do without that Swarajya and without a redress of those grievances. For me life would not be worth living if Ahmedabad continues to countenance violence in the name of truth. The poet has called Gujarat the "Garvi" (Great and Glorious) Gujarat. The Ahmedabad its capital is the residence of many religious Hindus and Muhammadans. Deeds of public violence in a city like this is like an ocean being on fire. Who can quench that fire? I can only offer myself as a sacrifice to be burnt in that fire, and I therefore ask you all to help in the attainment of the result that I desire out of my fast. May the love that lured you into unworthy acts awaken you to a sense of the reality, and if that love does continue to animate you, beware that I may not have to fast myself to death.

It seems that the deeds I have complained of have been done in an organised manner. There seems to be a definite design about them, and I am sure that there must be some educated and clever man or men behind them. They may be educated, but their education has not enlightened them. You have been misled into doing these deeds by such people. I advise you never to be so misguided, and I would ask them seriously to reconsider their views. To them and to you I commend my book "Hind Swarajya" which as I understand may be printed and published without infringing the law thereby.

Among the millhands the spinners have been on strike for some days. I advise them to resume work immediately and to ask for increase if they want any only after resuming work, and in a reasonable manner. To resort to the use of force to get any increase is suicidal. I would specially advise all millhands to altogether eschew violence. It is their interest to do so and I remind them of the promises made to Anasuya Bai and me that they would ever refrain from violence. I hope that all will now resume work.

MAHATMA GANDHI

Satyagraha (Noncoöperation) (1920)

On August 12, 1920, in Madras in south India, Gandhi addressed Hindus and Muslims on the practice of Satyagraha, or, as translated in this speech, "noncoöperation."

WHAT IS THIS noncoöperation, about which you have heard much, and why do we want to offer this noncoöperation? I wish to go for the time being into the why. There are two things before this country: the first and the foremost is the Khilafat question. On this the heart of the Mussalmans of India has become lascerated. British pledges given after the greatest deliberation by the Prime Minister of England in the name of the English nation, have been dragged into the mire. The promises given to Moslem India on the strength of which, the consideration that was expected by the British nation was exacted, have been broken, and the great religion of Islam has been placed in danger. The Mussalmans hold—and I venture to think they rightly hold—that so long as British promises remain unfulfilled, so long is it impossible for them to tender wholehearted fealty and loyalty to the British connection; and if it is to be a choice for a devout Mussalman between loyalty to the British connection and loyalty to his Code and Prophet, he will not require a second to make his choice,—and he has declared his choice. The Mussalmans say frankly openly and honourably to the whole world that if the British Ministers and the British nation do not fulfil the pledges given to them and do not wish to regard with respect the sentiments of 70 millions of the inhabitants of India who profess the faith of Islam, it will be impossible for them to retain Islamic loyalty. It is a question, then for the rest of the Indian population to consider whether they want to perform a neighbourly duty by their

99

Mussalman countrymen, and if they do, they have an opportunity of a lifetime which will not occur for another hundred years, to show their good-will, fellowship and friendship and to prove what they have been saying for all these long years that the Mussalman is the brother of the Hindu. If the Hindu regards that before the connection with the British nation comes his natural connection with his Moslem brother, then I say to you that if you find that the Moslem claim is just, that it is based upon real sentiment, and that at its background is this great religious feeling, you cannot do otherwise than help the Mussalman through and through, so long as their cause remains just, and the means for attaining the end remains equally just, honourable and free from harm to India. These are the plain conditions which the Indian Mussalmans have accepted; and it was when they saw that they could accept the proferred aid of the Hindus, that they could always justify the cause and the means before the whole world, that they decided to accept the proferred hand of fellowship. It is then for the Hindus and Mahomedans to offer a united front to the whole of the Christian powers of Europe and tell them that weak as India is, India has still got the capacity of preserving her self-respect, she still knows how to die for her religion and for her self-respect.

That is the Khilafat in a nut-shell; but you have also got the Punjab. The Punjab has wounded the heart of India as no other question has for the past century. I do not exclude from my calculation the Mutiny of 1857. Whatever hardships India had to suffer during the Mutiny, the insult that was attempted to be offered to her during the passage of the Rowlatt legislation and that which was offered after its passage were unparalleled in Indian history. It is because you want justice from the British nation in connection with the Punjab atrocities you have to devise, ways and means as to how you can get this justice. The House of Commons, the House of Lords, Mr. Montagu, the Viceroy of India, every one of them know what the feeling of India is on this Khilafat question and on that of the Punjab; the debates in both the Houses of Parliament, the action of Mr. Montagu and that of the Viceroy have demonstrated to you completely that they are not willing to give the justice which is India's due and which she demands. I suggest that our leaders have got to find a way out of this great difficulty and unless we have made ourselves even with the British rulers in India and unless we have gained a measure of self-respect at the hands of the British rulers in India, no connection, and no friendly intercourse is possible between them and ourselves. I, therefore, venture to suggest this beautiful and unanswerable method of noncoöperation.

I have been told that noncoöperation is unconstitutional. I venture to deny that it is unconstitutional. On the contrary, I hold that noncoöperation is a just and religious doctrine; it is the inherent right of every human being and it is perfectly constitutional. A great lover of the British Empire has said that under the British constitution even a successful rebellion is perfectly constitutional and he quotes historical instances, which I cannot deny, in support of his claim. I do not claim any constitutionality for a rebellion successful or otherwise, so long as that rebellion means in the ordinary sense of the term, what it does mean, namely wresting justice by violent means. On the contrary, I have said it repeatedly to my countrymen that violence whatever end it may serve in Europe, will never serve us in India. My brother and friend Shaukat Ali believes in methods of violence; and if it was in his power to draw the sword against the British Empire, I know that he has got the courage of a man and he has got also the wisdom to see that he should offer that battle to the British Empire. But because he recognises as a true soldier that means of violence are not open to India, he sides with me accepting my humble assistance and pledges his word that so long as I am with him and so long as he believes in the doctrine, so long will he not harbour even the idea of violence against any single Englishman or any single man on earth. I am here to tell you that he has been as true as his word and has kept it religiously. I am here to bear witness that he has been following out this plan of non-violent noncoöperation to the very letter and I am asking India to follow this non-violent noncoöperation. I tell you that there is not a better soldier living in our ranks in British India than Shaukat Ali. When the time for the drawing of the sword comes, if it ever comes, you will find him drawing that sword and you will find me retiring to the jungles of Hindustan. As soon as India accepts the doctrine of the sword, my life as an Indian is finished. It is because I believe in a mission special to India and it is because I believe that the ancients of India after centuries of experience have found out that the true thing for any human being on earth is not justice based on violence but justice based on sacrifice of self, justice based on Yagna and Kurbani,—I cling to that doctrine and I shall cling to it for ever,—it is for that reason I tell you that whilst my friend believes also in the doctrine of violence and has adopted the doctrine of non-violence as a weapon of the weak, I believe in the doctrine of non-violence as a weapon of the strongest. I believe that a man is the strongest soldier for daring to die unarmed with his breast bare before the enemy. So much for the non-violent part of noncoöperation. I, therefore, venture to suggest to my learned countrymen that so long as the doctrine of noncoöperation remains non-violent, so long there is nothing unconstitutional in that doctrine.

I ask further, is it unconstitutional for me to say to the British Government "I refuse to serve you"? Is it unconstitutional for our worthy Chairman to return with every respect all the titles that he has ever held from the Government? Is it unconstitutional for any parent to withdraw his children from a Government or aided school? Is it unconstitutional for a lawyer to say "I shall no longer support the arm of the law so long as that arm of law is used not to raise me but to debase me"? Is it unconstitutional for a civil servant or for a judge to say, "I refuse to serve a Government which does not wish to respect the wishes of the whole people"? I ask, is it unconstitutional for a policeman or for a soldier to tender his resignation when he knows that he is called to serve a Government which traduces its own countrymen"? Is it unconstitutional for me to go to the "krishan," to the agriculturist, and say to him "it is not wise for you to pay any taxes, if these taxes are used by the Government not to raise you but to weaken you"? I hold and I venture to submit, that there is nothing unconstitutional in it. What is more, I have done every one of these things in my life and nobody has questioned the constitutional character of it. I was in Kaira working in the midst of 7 lakhs of agriculturists. They had all suspended the payment of taxes and the whole of India was at one with me. Nobody considered that it was unconstitutional. I submit that in the whole plan of noncoöperation, there is nothing unconstitutional. But I do venture to suggest that it will be highly unconstitutional in the midst of this unconstitutional Government,—in the midst of a nation which has built up its magnificent constitution,—for the people of India to become weak and to crawl on their belly—it will be highly unconstitutional for the people of India to pocket every insult that is offered to them; it is highly unconstitutional for the 70 millions of Mahomedans of India to submit to a violent wrong done to their religion; it is highly unconstitutional for the whole of India to sit still and cooperate with an unjust Government which has trodden under its feet the honour of the Punjab. I say to my countrymen so long as you have a sense of honour and so long as you wish to remain the decendants and defenders of the noble traditions that have been handed to you for generations after generations, it is unconstitutional for you not to noncoöperate and unconstitutional for you to coöperate with a Government which has become so unjust as our Government has become. I am not anti-English; I am not anti-British; I am not anti any Government; but I am anti-untruth—anti-humbug and anti-injustice. So long as the Government spells injustice, it may regard me as its enemy, implacable enemy. I had hoped at the Congress at Amritsar—I am speaking God's truth before you—when I pleaded on bended knees before some of you for coöperation with the Government. I had full hope that the British Ministers who are wise, as a rule, would placate the Mussalman sentiment, that they would do full justice in the matter of the Punjab atrocities; and therefore, I said:—let us return good-will to the hand of fellowship that has been extended to us, which I then believed was extended to us through the Royal Proclamation. It was on that account that I pleaded for coöperation. But to-day that faith having gone and obliterated by the acts of the British Ministers, I am here to plead not for futile obstruction in the Legislative Council but for real substantial noncoöperation which would paralyse the mightiest Government on earth. That is what I stand for to-day. Until we have wrung Justice, and until we have wrung our self-respect from unwilling hands and from unwilling pens there can be no coöperation. Our Shastras say and I say so with the greatest deference to all the greatest religious preceptors of India but without fear of contradiction, that our Shastras teach us that there shall be no coöperation between injustice and justice, between an unjust man and a justice-loving man, between truth and untruth. Coöperation is a duty only so long as Government protects your honour, and non-coöperation is an equal duty when the Government instead of protecting robs you of your honour. That is the doctrine of non-coöperation.

I have been told that I should have waited for the declaration of the special Congress which is the mouthpiece of the whole nation. I know that it is the mouthpiece of the whole nation. If it was for me, individual Gandhi, to wait, I would have waited for eternity. But I had in my hands a sacred trust. I was advising my Mussalman countrymen and for the time being I hold their honour in my hands. I dare not ask them to wait for any verdict but the verdict of their own Conscience. Do you suppose that Mussalmans can eat their own words, can withdraw from the honourable position they have taken up? If perchance—and God forbid that it should happen—the Special Congress decides against them, I would still advise my countrymen, the Mussalmans to stand single handed and fight rather than yield to the attempted dishonour to their religion. It is therefore given to the Mussalmans to go to the Congress on bended knees and plead for support. But support or no support, it was not possible for them to wait for the Congress to give them the lead. They had to choose between futile violence, drawing of the naked sword and peaceful non-violent but effective noncoöperation, and they have made their choice. I venture further to say to you that if there is any body of men who feel as I do, the sacred character of noncoöperation, it is for you and me not to wait for the Congress but to act and to make it impossible for the Congress to give any other verdict. After all what is the Congress? The Congress is the collected voice of individuals who form it, and if the individuals go to the Congress with a united voice, that will be the verdict you will gain from the Congress. But if we go to the Congress with no opinion because we have none or because we are afraid to express it, then naturally we await the verdict of the Congress. To those who are unable to make up their mind I say, by all means wait. But for those who have seen the clear light as they see the lights in front of them, for them to wait is a sin. The Congress does not expect you to wait but it expects you to act so that the Congress can gauge properly the national feeling. So much for the Congress.

Among the details of noncoöperation I have placed in the foremost rank the boycott of the councils. Friends have quarrelled with me for the use of the word boycott, because I have disapproved—as I disapprove even now—boycott of British goods or any goods for that matter. But there, boycott has its own meaning and here boycott has its own meaning. I not only do not disapprove but approve of the boycott of the councils that are going to be formed next year. And why do I do it? The people—the masses,—require from us, the leaders, a clear lead. They do not want any equivocation from us. The suggestion that we should seek election and then refuse to take the oath of allegiance, would only make the nation distrust the leaders. It is not a clear lead to the nation. So I say to you, my countrymen, not to fall into this trap. We shall sell our country by adopting the method of seeking election and then not taking the oath of allegiance. We may find it difficult, and I frankly confess to you that I have not that trust in so many Indians making that declaration and standing by it. To-day I suggest to those who honestly hold the view—viz. that we should seek election and then refuse to take the oath of allegiance—I suggest to them that they will fall into a trap which they are preparing for themselves and for the nation. That is my view. I hold that if we want to give the nation the clearest possible lead, and if we want not to play with this great nation we must make it clear to this nation that we cannot take any favours, no matter how great they may be so long as those favours are accompanied by an injustice a double wrong done to India not yet redressed. The first indispensable thing before we can receive any favours from them is that they should redress this double wrong. There is a Greek proverb which used to say "Beware of the Greek but especially beware of them when they bring gifts to you." To-day from those ministers who are bent upon perpetuating the wrong to Islam and to the Punjab, I say we cannot accept gifts but we should be doubly careful lest we may not fall into the trap that they may have devised. I therefore suggest that we must not coquet with the council and must not have anything whatsoever to do with them. I am told that if we, who represent the national sentiment do not seek election, the Moderates who do not represent that sentiment will. I do not agree. I do not know what the Moderates represent and I do not know what the Nationalists represent. I know that there are good sheep and black sheep amongst the Moderates. I know that there are good sheep and black sheep amongst the Nationalists. I know that many Moderates hold honestly the view that it is a sin to resort to non-coöperation. I respectfully agree to differ from them. I do say to them also that they will fall into a trap which they will have devised if they seek election. But that does not affect my situation. If I feel in my heart of hearts that I ought not to go to the councils I ought at least to abide by this decision and it does not matter if ninety-nine other countrymen seek election. That is the only way in which public work can be done, and public opinion can be built. That is the only way in which reforms can be achieved and religion can be conserved. If it is a question of religious honour, whether I am one or among many I must stand upon my doctrine. Even if I should die in the attempt, it is worth dying for, than that I should live and deny my own doctrine. I suggest that it will be wrong on the part of any one to seek election to these Councils. If once we feel that we cannot cooperate with this Government, we have to commence from the top. We are the natural leaders of the people and we have acquired the right and the power to go to the nation and speak to it with the voice of noncoöperation. I therefore do suggest that it is inconsistent with noncoöperation to seek election to the Councils on any terms whatsoever.

I have suggested another difficult matter, viz., that the lawyers should suspend their practice. How should I do otherwise knowing so well how the Government had always been able to retain this power through the instrumentality of lawyers. It is perfectly true that it is the lawyers of today who are leading us, who are fighting the country's battles, but when it comes to a matter of action against the Government, when it comes to a matter of paralysing the activity of the Government I know that the Government always look to the lawyers, however fine fighters they may have been, to preserve their dignity and their self-respect. I therefore suggest to my lawyer friends that it is their duty to suspend their practice and to show to the Government that they will no longer retain their offices, because lawyers are considered to be honorary officers of the courts and therefore subject to their disciplinary jurisdiction. They must no longer retain these honorary offices if they want to withdraw coöperation from Government. But what will happen to law and order? We shall evolve law and order through the instrumentality of these very lawyers. We shall promote arbitration courts and dispense justice, pure, simple, home-made justice, swadeshi justice to our countrymen. That is what suspension of practice means.

I have suggested yet another difficulty—to withdraw our children from the Government schools and to ask collegiate students to withdraw from the College and to empty Government aided schools. How could I do otherwise? I want to gauge the national sentiment. I want to know whether the Mahomedans feel deeply. If they feel deeply they will understand in the twinkling of an eye, that it is not right for them to receive schooling from a Government in which they have lost all faith; and which they do not trust at all. How can I, if I do not want to help this Government, receive any help from that Government. I think that the schools and colleges are factories for making clerks and Government servants. I would not help this great factory for manufacturing clerks and servants if I want to withdraw coöperation from that Government. Look at it from any point of view you like. It is not possible for you to send your children to the schools and still believe in the doctrine of noncoöperation.

I have gone further. I have suggested that our title holders should give up their titles. How can they hold on to the titles and honours bestowed by this Government? They were at one time badges of honour when we believed that national honour was safe in their hands. But now they are no longer badges of honour but badges of dishonour and disgrace when we really believe that we cannot get justice from this Government. Every title holder holds his titles and honours as trustee for the nation and in this first step in the withdrawal of coöperation from the Government they should surrender their titles without a moment's consideration. I suggest to my Mahomedan countrymen that if they fail in this primary duty they will certainly fail in noncoöperation unless the masses themselves reject the classes and take up noncoöperation in their own hands and are able to fight that battle even as the men of the French Revolution were able to take the reins of Government in their own hands leaving aside the leaders and marched to the banner of victory. I want no revolution. I want ordered progress. I want no disordered order. I want no chaos. I want real order to be evolved out of this chaos which is misrepresented to me as order. If it is order established by a tyrant in order to get hold of the tyrannical reins of Government I say that it is no order for me but it is disorder. I want to evolve justice out of this injustice. Therefore I suggest to you the passive noncoöperation. If we would only realise the secret of this peaceful and infallible doctrine you will know and you will find that you will not want to use even an angry word when they lift the sword at you and you will not want even to lift your little finger, let alone a stick or a sword.

You may consider that I have spoken these words in anger because I have considered the ways of this Government immoral, unjust, debasing and untruthful. I use these adjectives with the greatest deliberation. I have used them for my own true brother with whom I was engaged in a battle of noncoöperation for full 13 years and although the ashes cover the remains of my brother I tell you that I used to tell him that he was unjust when his plans were based upon immoral foundation. I used to tell him that he did not stand for truth. There was no anger in me. I told him this home truth because I loved him. In the same manner, I tell the British people that I love them, and that I want their association but I want that association on conditions well defined. I want my self-respect and I want my absolute equality with them. If I cannot gain that equality from the British people, I do not want that British connection. If I have to let the British people go and import temporary disorder and dislocation of national business, I will favour that disorder and dislocation than that I should have injustice from the hands of a great nation such as the British nation. You will find that by the time the whole chapter is closed that the successors of Mr. Montagu will give me the credit for having rendered the most distinguished service that I have yet rendered to the Empire, in having offered this noncoöperation and in having suggested the boycott; not of His Royal Highness the Prince of Wales, but of boycott of a visit engineered by the Government in order to tighten its hold on the national neck. I will not allow it even if I stand alone, if I cannot persuade this nation not to welcome that visit but will boycott that visit with all the power at my command. It is for that reason I stand before you and implore you to offer this religious battle, but it is not a battle offered to you by a visionary or a saint. I deny being a visionary. I do not accept the claim of saintliness. I am of the earth, earthy, a common gardener man as much as any one of you, probably much more than you are. I am prone to as many weaknesses as you are. But I have seen the world. I have lived in the world with my eyes open. I have gone through the most fiery ordeals that have fallen to the lot of man. I have gone through this discipline. I have understood the secret of my own sacred Hinduism. I have learnt the lesson that noncoöperation is the duty not merely of the saint but it is the duty of every ordinary citizen, who not knowing much, not caring to know much but wants to perform his ordinary household functions. The people of Europe teach even their masses, the poor people the doctrine of the sword. But the Rishis of India, those who have held the traditions of India have preached to the masses of India the doctrine, not of the sword, not of violence but of suffering, of self-suffering. And unless you and I am prepared to go through this primary lesson we are not ready even to offer the sword and that is the lesson my brother Shaukat Ali has imbibed to teach and that is why he to-day accepts my advice tendered to him in all prayerfulness and in all humility and says "long live noncoöperation." Please remember that even in England the little children were withdrawn from the schools; and colleges in Cambridge and Oxford were closed. Lawyers had left their desks and were fighting in the trenches. I do not present to you the trenches but I do ask you to go through the sacrifice that the men, women and the brave lads of England went through. Remember that you are offering battle to a nation which is saturated with the spirit of sacrifice whenever the occasion arises. Remember that the little band of Boers offered stubborn resistance to a mighty nation. But their lawyers had left their desks. Their mothers had withdrawn their children from the schools and colleges and the children had become the volunteers of the nation. I have seen them with these naked eyes of mine. I am asking my country-men in India to follow no other gospel than the gospel of self-sacrifice which precedes every battle. Whether you belong to the school of violence or non-violence you will still have to go through the fire of sacrifice, and of discipline. May God grant you, may God grant our leaders, the wisdom, the courage and the true knowledge to lead the nation to its cherished goal. May God grant the people of India the right path, the true vision and the ability and the courage to follow this path, difficult and yet easy, of sacrifice.

MAHATMA GANDHI

Limitations of Satyagraha (1927)

Gandhi describes civil disobedience as a subset of Satyagraha ("All Civil Disobedience is a part or branch of Satyagraha, but all Satyagraha is not Civil Disobedience"), and then offers a civil disobedience challenge to a Satyagrahi, one more "pure" than he.

ALL CIVIL DISOBEDIENCE is a part or branch of Satyagraha, but all Satyagraha is not Civil Disobedience. And seeing that the Nagpur friends have suspended what they were pleased to call Satyagraha or Civil Disobedience, let me suggest for their information and that of others how Satyagraha can be legitimately offered with reference to the Bengal detenus. If they will not be angry with me or laugh at me, let me commence by saying that they can offer Satyagraha by developing the power of the people through *khadi,* and through *khadi* achieving boycott of foreign cloth. They can offer Satyagraha by becoming precursors of Hindu-Muslim unity, by allowing their heads to be broken whenever there is a quarrel between the two, and whilst there is no active quarrel in their parts by performing silent acts of service to those of the opposite faith to theirs. If such constructive methods are too flat for them, and if they will be satisfied by nothing less than Civil Disobedience in spite of the violence of thought, word and deed raging round us, I suggest the following prescription of individual Civil Disobedience, which even one man can offer, not indeed in the hope of securing immediate release of detenus, but certainly in the hope of the individual sacrifice ultimately eventuating in such release. Let a batch, or only one person, say from Nagpur, march on foot to the Government House in Calcutta, and if a march is irksome or impossible then let him, her, or them beg enough money for trainfare from friends, and having reached Calcutta let only one Satyagrahi march to the Government House and walk on to the point where he or she is stopped. There let him or her stop

and demand the release of detenus or his or her own arrest. To preserve intact the civil nature of this disobedience the Satyagrahi must
be wholly unarmed, and in spite of insults, kicks or worse must
meekly stand the ground, and be arrested without the slightest opposition. He may carry his own food in his pocket, a bottleful of water,
take his *Gita,* the Koran, the Bible, the Zend Avesta or the Granth
Sahib, as the case may be, and his *takli.* If there are many such real
Satyagrahis, they will certainly transform the atmosphere in an
immensely short time, even as one gentle shower transforms the
plains of India into a beautiful green carpet in one single day.

The question will legitimately be asked, 'If you really mean what
you say, why don't you take the lead, never mind whether any one
follows you or not?' My answer is: I do not regard myself as pure
enough to undertake such a heroic mission. I am trying every
moment of my life to attain the requisite purity of thought, word
and deed. As it is, I confess that I am swayed by many passions.
Anger wells up in my breast when I see or hear about what I consider to be misdeeds. All I can humbly claim for myself is that I can
keep these passions and moods under fair subjection, and prevent
them from gaining mastery over me. But the standard of purity that
I want, for any such heroic measure is not to have such passions at
all and yet to hate the wrong. When I feel that I have become
incapable even of thinking evil, and I hold it to be possible for
every God-fearing man to attain that state, I shall wait for no man's
advice, and even at the risk of being called the maddest of men, I
shall not hesitate to knock at the Viceregal gate or go wherever
God leads me, and demand what is due to this country which is
being ground to dust today.

Meanwhile let no man mock at Satyagraha. Let no man parody it.
If it is at all possible, leave Satyagraha alone, and the whole field is
open for unchecked action. On a chartless sea in which there is no
light-house a captain dares whither he wills. But a captain who
knowing the existence of a light-house and its position, sails anyhow,
or takes no precaution for knowing the light-house from deceiving
stars, will be considered unfit for his post. If the reader can bear with
me, let him understand that I claim to be the keeper of the
light-house called Satyagraha in the otherwise chartless sea of Indian
politics. And, therefore, it is that I have suggested, that those who
make for Satyagraha will do well to go to its keeper. But I know that
I have no patent rights in Satyagraha. I can, therefore, merely rely
upon the indulgence of fellow-workers for recognition of my office.

MAHATMA GANDHI

On the Eve of the March (1930)

Gandhi's "Salt March" was one of history's most famous and daring acts of civil disobedience. He explains herein the perversity of the British tax on salt that oppressed every impoverished Indian in the country. He set out on a 240-mile march to the sea and arrived a month later, with sympathizers joining him, in early April. Tens of thousands of civilly disobedient participants that year were arrested, including Gandhi, whose "Message to the Nation" (below) anticipated that arrest.

IN ALL PROBABILITY this will be my last speech to you. Even if the Government allow me to march tomorrow morning, this will be my last speech on the sacred banks of the Sabarmati. Possibly these may be the last words of my life here.

I have already told you yesterday what I had to say. Today I shall confine myself to what you should do after my companions and I are arrested. The programme of the march to Jalalpur must be fulfilled as originally settled. The enlistment of volunteers for this purpose should be confined to Gujarat. From what I have seen and heard during the last fortnight, I am inclined to believe that the stream of civil resisters will flow unbroken.

But let there be not a semblance of breach of peace even after all of us have been arrested. We have resolved to utilize all our resources in the pursuit of an exclusively non-violent struggle. Let no one commit a wrong in anger. This is my hope and prayer. I wish these words of mine reached every nook and corner of the land. My task shall be done if I perish and so do my comrades. It will then be for the Working Committee of the Congress to show you the way and it will be up to you to follow its lead. That is the only meaning of the Working Committee's resolution. The reins of the movement will still remain in the hands of those of my associates who believe in non-violence as an article of faith. Of course, the Congress will be free to chalk out what course of action commends itself to it. So long as I have not reached Jalalpur, let nothing be done in contravention to the authority vested in me by the Congress. But once I am arrested, the whole general responsibility shifts to the Congress. No one who believes in non-violence, as a creed, need therefore sit still. My compact with the Congress ends as soon as I am arrested. In that case there should be no slackness in the enrolment of volunteers. Wherever possible, civil disobedience of Salt laws should be started. These laws can be violated in three ways. It is an offence to manufacture salt wherever there are facilities for doing so. The possession and sale of contraband salt (which includes natural salt or salt earth) is also an offence. The purchasers of such salt will be equally guilty. To carry away the natural salt deposits on the sea-shore is likewise a violation of law. So is the hawking of such salt. In short, you may choose any one or all of these devices to break the salt monopoly.

We are, however, not to be content with this alone. Wherever there are Congress Committees, wherever there is no ban by the Congress and wherever the local workers have self-confidence, other suitable measures may be adopted. I prescribe only one condition, viz., let our pledge of truth and non-violence as the only means for the attainment of Swaraj be faithfully kept. For the rest, every one has a free hand. But that does not give a licence to all and sundry to carry on on their individual responsibility. Wherever there are local leaders, their orders should be obeyed by the people. Where there are no leaders and only a handful of men have faith in the programme, they may do what they can, if they have enough self-confidence. They have a right, nay it is their duty, to do so. The history of the world is full of instances of men who rose to leadership by sheer force of self-confidence, bravery and tenacity. We too, if we sincerely aspire to Swaraj and are impatient to attain it, should have similar self-confidence. Our ranks will swell and our hearts strengthen as the number of our arrests by Government increases.

Let nobody assume that after I am arrested there will be no one left to guide you. It is not I but Pandit Jawaharlal who is your guide. He has the capacity to lead. Though the fact is that those who have learnt the lesson of fearlessness and self-effacement need no leader. If we lack these virtues, not even Jawaharlal will be able to produce them in us.

Much can be done in other ways besides these. Liquor and foreign cloth shops can be picketed. We can refuse to pay taxes if we have the requisite strength. The lawyers can give up practice. The public can boycott the Courts by refraining from litigation. Government servants can resign their posts. In the midst of the despair reigning all round people quake with fear of losing employment. Such men are unfit for Swaraj. But why this despair? The number of Government servants in the country does not exceed a few hundred thousand. What about the rest? Where are they to go? Even free India will not be able to accommodate a greater number of public servants. A Collector then will not need the number of servants he has got today. He will be his own servant. How can a poor country like India afford to provide a Collector with separate servants for performing the duties of carrying his papers, sweeping, cooking, latrine cleaning and letter carrying? Our starving millions can by no means afford this enormous expenditure. If, therefore, we are sensible enough, let us bid good-bye to Government employment, no matter if it is the post of a judge or a peon. It may be difficult for a judge to leave his job, but where is the difficulty in the case of a peon? He can earn his bread everywhere by honest manual labour. This is the easiest solution of the problem of freedom: Let all who are co-operating with the Government in one way or another, be it by paying taxes, keeping titles, or sending children to official schools etc., withdraw their co-operation in all or as many ways as possible. One can devise other methods too of non-co-operating with the Government. And then there are women who can stand shoulder to shoulder with men in this struggle.

You may take it as my will. It was the only message that I desired to impart to you before starting on the march or for the jail. I wish that there should be no suspension or abandonment of the war that commences tomorrow morning, or earlier if I am arrested before that time. I shall eagerly await the news that ten batches are ready as soon as my batch is arrested. I believe there are men in India to complete the work begun by me today. I have faith in the righteousness of our cause and the purity of our weapons. And where the means are clean, there God is undoubtedly present with His blessings. And where these three combine, there defeat is an impossibility. A Satyagrahi, whether free or incarcerated, is ever victorious. He is vanquished only when he forsakes truth and non-violence and turns a deaf ear to the Inner Voice. If, therefore, there is such a thing as defeat for even a Satyagrahi, he alone is the cause of it. God bless you all and keep off all obstacles from the path in the struggle that begins tomorrow. Let this be our prayer.

MAHATMA GANDHI

Message to the Nation (1930)

Gandhi's "Salt March" campaign brought worldwide attention to the injustices of British rule in India. Gandhi was jailed until January 1931.

AT LAST THE long expected hour seems to have come.

In the dead of night my colleagues and companions have roused me from deep slumber and requested me to give them a message. I am therefore dictating this message, although I have not the slightest inclination to give any.

Messages I have given enough already. Of what avail would this message be if none of the previous messages evoked a proper response? But information received until this midnight leads me to the belief that my message did not fall flat, but was taken up by the people in right earnest.

The people of Gujarat seem to have risen in a body as it were. I have seen with my own eyes thousands of men and women at Aat and Bhimrad, fearlessly breaking the Salt Act. Not a sign of mischief, not a sign of violence have I seen, despite the presence of people in such large numbers. They have remained perfectly peaceful and nonviolent, although Government officers have transgressed all bounds.

Here in Gujarat well-tried and popular public servants have been arrested one after another, and yet the people have been perfectly non-violent. They have refused to give way to panic, and have celebrated the arrests, by offering civil disobedience in ever increasing numbers. This is just as it should be.

If the struggle auspiciously begun is continued in the same spirit of non-violence to the end, not only shall we see *Purna Swaraj* established in our country before long, but we shall have given to the world an object lesson worthy of India and her glorious past.

Swaraj won without sacrifice cannot last long. I would therefore like our people to get ready to make the highest sacrifice that they are capable of. In true sacrifice all the suffering is on one side—one is required to master the art of getting killed without killing, of gaining life by losing it. May India live up to this *mantra*.

At present India's self-respect, in fact her all, is symbolized as it were in a handful of salt in the Satyagrahi's hand. Let the fist holding it, therefore, be broken, but let there be no voluntary surrender of the salt.

Let the Government, if it claims to be a civilized Government, jail those who help themselves to contraband salt. After their arrest the civil resisters will gladly surrender the salt, as they will their bodies into the custody of their jailors.

But by main force to snatch the salt from the poor, harmless Satyagrahis' hands is barbarism pure and simple and an insult to India. Such insult can be answered only by allowing our hand to be fractured without loosening the grasp. Even then the actual sufferer or his comrades may not harbour in their hearts anger against the wrongdoer. Incivility should be answered not by incivility but by a dignified and calm endurance of all suffering in the name of God.

Let not my companions or the people at large be perturbed over my arrest, for it is not I, but God who is guiding this movement. He ever dwells in the hearts of all and He will vouchsafe to us the right guidance if only we have faith in Him. Our path has already been chalked out for us. Let every village fetch or manufacture contraband salt. Sisters should picket liquor shops, opium dens and foreign-cloth dealers' shops. Young and old in every home should ply the *takli* and spin and get woven heaps of yarn every day. Foreign cloth should be burnt. Hindus should eschew untouchability. Hindus, Mussalmans, Sikhs, Parsis, and Christians should all achieve heart unity. Let the majority rest content with what remains after the minorities have been satisfied. Let students leave Government schools and colleges, and Government servants resign their service and devote themselves to service of the people, and we shall find that *Purna Swaraj* will come knocking at our doors.

ALBERT EINSTEIN

The "Two Percent" Speech (1930)

The renowned theoretical physicist Albert Einstein (1879–1955) was born in Germany but gave up his citizenship as a teenager so that he would not have to serve in the army. He later returned, however, to direct the prestigious physics institute at the University of Berlin, where during World War I he expressed his disgust at warfare: "Europe, in her insanity, has started something unbelievable. In such times one realizes to what a sad species of animal one belongs."[1] He won the Nobel Prize in Physics for 1921, but as the Nazis gained power over that decade, he was regularly denounced and threatened, usually simply for being Jewish; he emigrated to the United States in 1933. Though a committed pacifist, by the late 1930s he found himself involved in spurring America to develop an atomic bomb to counter Nazi Germany's development of one. "In fact," writes Otto Nathan, "Einstein believed he served the cause of pacifism, as he understood it, when he called for the rearmament of the West against the menace of Nazism; he felt there was a better chance of avoiding war if Germany knew that the Western countries were militarily prepared in the event of conflict."[2]

After World War II, Einstein argued against the proliferation of nuclear weapons. He was often called upon to speak on his moral beliefs; the editors Otto Nathan and Heinz Norden have explained the context of this selection's particular occasion: "A climactic point in Einstein's career as a militant pacifist came on December 14, 1930, when he spoke at a meeting in New York's Ritz-Carlton Hotel, under the auspices of the New History Society. The speech was delivered extemporaneously, and when the interpreter originally designated proved unequal to the task, Mrs. Rosika Schwimmer volunteered to translate Einstein's remarks into English."[3] The particular remark that gave this speech its name is this: "Even if only two per cent of those

---

[1] Albert Einstein. *Einstein on Peace*. Edited by Otto Nathan and Heinz Norden. New York: Schocken Books. 1968. 2.

[2] *Ibid.* x.

[3] *Ibid.* 116.

assigned to perform military service should announce their refusal to fight, as well as urge means other than war of settling international disputes, governments would be powerless, they would not dare send such a large number of people to jail."

WHEN THOSE WHO are bound together by pacifist ideals hold a meeting they are usually consorting only with their own kind. They are like sheep huddled together while wolves wait outside. I believe that pacifist speakers face this difficulty: they ordinarily reach only their own group, people who are pacifists anyhow and hardly need to be convinced. The sheep's voice does not reach beyond this circle and is, therefore, ineffectual. That is the real weakness of the pacifist movement.

Genuine pacifists, those whose heads are not in the clouds but who think in realistic terms, must fearlessly endeavor to act in a manner which is of practical value to the cause rather than remain content merely to espouse the ideals of pacifism. Deeds, not words, are needed; mere words get pacifists nowhere. They must initiate action and begin with what can be achieved now.

As to what our next step should be, I should like you to realize that under the present military system every man is compelled to commit the crime of killing for his country. The aim of all pacifists must be to convince others of the immorality of war and rid the world of the shameful slavery of military service. I wish to suggest two ways to achieve that aim.

The first has already been put into practice: uncompromising war resistance and refusal to do military service under any circumstances. In countries where conscription exists, the true pacifist must refuse military duty. Already, a considerable number of pacifists in many countries have refused and are refusing, at great personal sacrifice, to serve a military term in peacetime. By doing so, it becomes manifest that they will not fight in the event of war.

In countries where compulsory service does not exist, true pacifists must publicly declare in time of peace that they will not take up arms under any circumstances. This, too, is an effective method of war resistance. I earnestly urge you to try to convince people all over the world of the justice of this position. The timid may say, "What is the use? We shall be sent to prison." To them I would reply: Even if only two per cent of those assigned to perform military service should announce their refusal to fight, as well as urge means other than war of settling international disputes, governments would be powerless, they would not dare send such a large number of people to jail.

A second line of action for war resisters, which I suggest, is a policy which would not involve personal involvement with the law. That is, to try to establish through international legislation the right to refuse military service in peacetime. Those who are unwilling to accept such a position might prefer to advocate legislation which would permit them, in place of military service, to do some strenuous or even dangerous work, in the interest of their own country or of mankind as a whole. They would thereby prove that their war resistance is unselfish and merely a logical consequence of the belief that international differences can be settled in ways other than fighting; it would further prove that their opposition to war could not be attributed to cowardice or the desire for personal comfort or unwillingness to serve their country or humanity. If we declare our willingness to accept work of a dangerous nature, we shall have advanced far on the road to a more peaceful world.

I further suggest that pacifists of all countries start raising funds to support those who would want to refuse military service but who cannot actually do so for lack of financial means. I, therefore, advocate the establishment of an international organization and an international pacifist fund to support the active war resisters of our day.

In conclusion, may I say that the serious pacifists who want to accomplish peace must have the courage to initiate and to carry on these aims; only then will the world be obliged to take notice. Pacifists will then be heard by people who are not already pacifists; and once they are listened to, their message is bound to be effective. If they are too restrained, their voices will continue to reach only those in their own circle. They will remain sheep, pacifist sheep.

MARTIN LUTHER KING, JR.

Love, Law, and Civil Disobedience (1961)

Inspired by Mohandas Gandhi and Henry David Thoreau, the Baptist minister Dr. Martin Luther King, Jr. (1929–1968), was the most influential proponent of civil rights in American history. He advocated for social change through civil disobedience in his protests against discriminatory and racist laws in the American South during the 1950s and 1960s. In "Love, Law, and Civil Disobedience," a transcript of the speech he delivered to the Fellowship of the Concerned on November 16, 1961, King spoke out for justice with an unmatched focus, passion and power in his attempt to persuade that committee to hasten its efforts against segregation. He hailed the resolute student movement that participated in the Freedom Rides in Jackson, Mississippi: "They may even face physical death, and yet they could sing, 'We shall overcome.' Most of them realized that they would be thrown into jail, and yet they could sing, 'We shall overcome, we are not afraid.' Then something caused me to see at that moment the real meaning of the movement. That students had faith in the future. That the movement was based on hope, that this movement had something within it that says somehow even though the arc of the moral universe is long, it bends toward justice."

MEMBERS OF THE Fellowship of the Concerned, of the Southern Regional Council, I need not pause to say how very delighted I am to be here today, and to have the opportunity of being a little part of this very significant gathering. I certainly want to express my personal appreciation to Mrs. Tilly and the members of the Committee, for giving me this opportunity. I would also like to express just a personal word of thanks and appreciation for your vital witness in this period of transition which we are facing in our Southland, and in the nation, and I am sure that as a result of this genuine concern, and your significant work in communities all across the South, we have a better South today and I am sure will have a better South tomorrow with your continued endeavor and I do want to express my personal gratitude and appreciation to you of the Fellowship of the Concerned for your significant work and for your forthright witness.

Now, I have been asked to talk about the philosophy behind the student movement. There can be no gainsaying of the fact that we confront a crisis in race relations in the United States. This crisis has been precipitated on the one hand by the determined resistance of reactionary forces in the South to the Supreme Court's decision in 1954 outlawing segregation in the public schools. And we know that at times this resistance has risen to ominous proportions. At times we find the legislative halls of the South ringing loud with such words as interposition and nullification. And all of these forces have developed into massive resistance. But we must also say that the crisis has been precipitated on the other hand by the determination of hundreds and thousands and millions of Negro people to achieve freedom and human dignity. If the Negro stayed in his place and accepted discrimination and segregation, there would be no crisis. But the Negro has a new sense of dignity, a new self-respect and new determination. He has reevaluated his own intrinsic worth. Now this new sense of dignity on the part of the Negro grows out of the same longing for freedom and human dignity on the part of the oppressed people all over the world; for we see it in Africa, we see it in Asia, and we see it all over the world. Now we must say that this struggle for freedom will not come to an automatic halt, for history reveals to us that once oppressed people rise up against that oppression, there is no stopping point short of full freedom. On the other hand, history reveals to us that those who oppose the movement for freedom are those who are in privileged positions who very seldom give up their privileges without strong resistance. And they very seldom do it voluntarily. So the sense of struggle will continue. The question is how will the struggle be waged.

Now there are three ways that oppressed people have generally dealt with their oppression. One way is the method of acquiescence, the method of surrender; that is, the individuals will somehow adjust themselves to oppression, they adjust themselves to discrimination or to segregation or colonialism or what have you. The other method that has been used in history is that of rising up against the oppressor with corroding hatred and physical violence. Now of course we know about this method in Western civilization because in a sense it has been the hall-mark of its grandeur, and the inseparable twin of western materialism. But there is a weakness in this method because it ends up creating many more social problems than it solves. And I am convinced that if the Negro succumbs to the temptation of using violence in his struggle for freedom and justice, unborn generations will be the recipients of a long and desolate night of bitterness. And our chief legacy to the future will be an endless reign of meaningless chaos.

But there is another way, namely the way of nonviolent resistance. This method was popularized in our generation by a little man from India, whose name was Mohandas K. Gandhi. He used this method in a magnificent way to free his people from the economic exploitation and the political domination inflicted upon them by a foreign power.

This has been the method used by the student movement in the South and all over the United States. And naturally whenever I talk about the student movement I cannot be totally objective. I have to be somewhat subjective because of my great admiration for what the students have done. For in a real sense they have taken our deep groans and passionate yearnings for freedom, and filtered them in their own tender souls, and fashioned them into a creative protest which is an epic known all over our nation. As a result of their disciplined, nonviolent, yet courageous struggle, they have been able to do wonders in the South, and in our nation. But this movement does have an underlying philosophy, it has certain ideas that are attached to it, it has certain philosophical precepts. These are the things that I would like to discuss for the few moments left.

I would say that the first point or the first principle in the movement is the idea that means must be as pure as the end. This movement is based on the philosophy that ends and means must cohere. Now this has been one of the long struggles in history, the whole idea of means and ends. Great philosophers have grappled with it, and sometimes they have emerged with the idea, from Machiavelli on down, that the end justifies the means. There is a great system of thought in our world today, known as communism. And I think that with all of the weakness and tragedies of communism, we find its greatest tragedy right here, that it goes under the philosophy that the end justifies the means that are used in the process. So we can read or we can hear the Lenins say that lying, deceit, or violence, that many of these things justify the ends of the classless society.

This is where the student movement and the nonviolent movement that is taking place in our nation would break with communism and any other system that would argue that the end justifies the means. For in the long run, we must see that the end represents the means in process and the ideal in the making. In other words, we cannot believe, or we cannot go with the idea that the end justifies the means because the end is preexistent in the means. So the idea of nonviolent resistance, the philosphy of nonviolent resistance, is the philosophy which says that the means must be as pure as the end, that in the long run of history, immoral destructive means cannot bring about moral and constructive ends.

There is another thing about this philosophy, this method of nonviolence which is followed by the student movement. It says that those who adhere to or follow this philosophy must follow a consistent principle of noninjury. They must consistently refuse to inflict injury upon another. Sometimes you will read the literature of the student movement and see that, as they are getting ready for the sit-in or stand-in, they will read something like this, "If you are hit do not hit back, if you are cursed do not curse back." This is the whole idea, that the individual who is engaged in a nonviolent struggle must never inflict injury upon another. Now this has an external aspect and it has an internal one. From the external point of view it means that the individuals involved must avoid external physical violence. So they don't have guns, they don't retaliate with physical violence. If they are hit in the process, they avoid external physical violence at every point. But it also means that they avoid internal violence of spirit. This is why the love ethic stands so high in the student movement. We have a great deal of talk about love and nonviolence in this whole thrust.

Now when the students talk about love, certainly they are not talking about emotional bosh, they are not talking about merely a sentimental outpouring; they're talking something much deeper, and I always have to stop and try to define the meaning of love in this context. The Greek language comes to our aid in trying to deal with this. There are three words in the Greek language for love; one is the word *eros*. This is a beautiful type of love, it is an aesthetic love. Plato talks about it a great deal in his Dialogue, the yearning of the soul for the realm of the divine. It has come to us to be a sort of romantic love, and so in a sense we have read about it and experienced it. We've read about it in all the beauties of literature. I guess in a sense Edgar Allan Poe was talking about *eros* when he talked about his beautiful Annabelle [*sic*] Lee, with the love surrounded by the halo of eternity. In a sense Shakespeare was talking about *eros* when he said "Love is not love which alters when it alteration finds, or bends with the remover to remove; O'no! It is an ever fixed mark that looks on tempests and is never shaken, it is the star to every wandering bark." (You know, I remember that because I used to quote it to this little lady when we were courting; that's *eros*.) The Greek language talks about *philia* which was another level of love. It is an intimate affection between personal friends, it is a reciprocal love. On this level you love because you are loved. It is friendship.

Then the Greek language comes out with another word which is called the *agape*. *Agape* is more than romantic love, *agape* is more than friendship. *Agape* is understanding, creative, redemptive, good will to all men. It is an overflowing love which seeks nothing in return. Theologians would say that it is the love of God operating in the human heart. So that when one rises to love on this level, he loves men not because he likes them, not because their ways appeal to him, but he loves every man because God loves him. And he rises to the point of loving the person who does an evil deed while hating the deed that the person does. I think this is what Jesus meant when he said "love your enemies." I'm very happy that he didn't say like your enemies, because it is pretty difficult to like some people. Like is sentimental, and it is pretty difficult to like someone bombing your home; it is pretty difficult to like somebody threatening your children; it is difficult to like congressmen who spend all of their time trying to defeat civil rights. But Jesus says love them, and love is greater than like. Love is understanding, redemptive, creative, good will for all men. And it is this idea, it is this whole ethic of love which is the idea standing at the basis of the student movement.

There is something else: that one seeks to defeat the unjust system, rather than individuals who are caught in that system. And that one goes on believing that somehow this is the important thing, to get rid of the evil system and not the individual who happens to be misguided, who happens to be misled, who was taught wrong. The thing to do is to get rid of the system and thereby create a moral balance within society. Another thing that stands at the center of this movement is another idea: that suffering can be a most creative and powerful social force. Suffering has certain moral attributes involved, but it can be a powerful and creative social force. Now, it is very interesting at this point to notice that both violence and nonviolence agree that suffering can be a very powerful social force. But there is this difference: violence says that suffering can be a powerful social force by inflicting the suffering on somebody else: so this is what we do in war, this is what we do in the whole violent thrust of the violent movement. It believes that you achieve some end by inflicting suffering on another. The nonviolent say that suffering becomes a powerful social force when you willingly accept that violence on yourself, so that self-suffering stands at the center of the nonviolent movement and the individuals involved are able to suffer in a creative manner, feeling that unearned suffering is redemptive, and that suffering may serve to transform the social situation.

Another thing in this movement is the idea that there is within human nature an amazing potential for goodness. There is within human nature something that can respond to goodness. I know somebody's liable to say that this is an unrealistic movement if it goes on believing that all people are good. Well, I didn't say that. I think the students are realistic enough to believe that there is a strange dichotomy of disturbing dualism within human nature. Many of the great philosophers and thinkers through the ages have seen this. It caused Ovid the Latin poet to say, "I see and approve the better things of life, but the evil things I do." It caused even Saint Augustine to say "Lord, make me pure, but not yet." So that that is in human nature. Plato, centuries ago said that the human personality is like a charioteer with two headstrong horses, each wanting to go in different directions, so that within our own individual lives we see this conflict and certainly when we come to the collective life of man, we see a strange badness. But in spite of this there is something in human nature that can respond to goodness. So that man is neither innately good nor is he innately bad; he has potentialities for both. So in this sense, Carlyle was right when he said that, "there are depths in man which go down to the lowest hell, and heights which reach the highest heaven, for are not both heaven and hell made but of him, ever-lasting miracle and mystery that he is?" Man has the capacity to be good, man has the capacity to be evil.

And so the nonviolent resister never lets this idea go, that there is something within human nature than can respond to goodness. So that a Jesus of Nazareth or a Mohandas Gandhi, can appeal to human beings and appeal to that element of goodness within them, and a Hitler can appeal to the element of evil within them. But we must never forget that there is something within human nature that can respond to goodness, that man is not totally depraved; to put it in theological terms, the image of God is never totally gone. And so the individuals who believe in this movement and who believe in nonviolence and our struggle in the South, somehow believe that even the worst segrationist can become an integrationist. Now sometimes it is hard to believe that this is what this movement says, and it believes it firmly, that there is something within human nature that can be changed, and this stands at the top of the whole philosophy of the student movement and the philosophy of non-violence.

It says something else. It says that it is as much a moral obligation to refuse to cooperate with evil as it is to cooperate with good. Noncooperation with evil is as much a moral obligation as the cooperation with good. So that the student movement is willing to stand up courageously on the idea of civil disobedience. Now I think this is the part of the student movement that is probably mis-understood more than anything else. And it is a difficult aspect, because on the one hand the students would say, and I would say, and all the people who believe in civil rights would say, obey the Supreme Court's decision of 1954 and at the same time, we would disobey certain laws that exist on the statutes of the South today.

This brings in the whole question of how can you be logically consistent when you advocate obeying some laws and disobeying other laws. Well, I think one would have to see the whole meaning of this movement at this point by seeing that the students recognize that there are two types of laws. There are just laws and there are unjust laws. And they would be the first to say obey the just laws, they would be the first to say that men and women have a moral obligation to obey just and right laws. And they would go on to say that we must see that there are unjust laws. Now the question comes into being, what is the difference, and who determines the difference, what is the difference between a just and an unjust law?

Well, a just law is a law that squares with a moral law. It is a law that squares with that which is right, so that any law that uplifts human personality is a just law. Whereas that law which is out of harmony with the moral is a law which does not square with the moral law of the universe. It does not square with the law of God, so for that reason it is unjust and any law that degrades the human personality is an unjust law. Well, somebody says that that does not mean anything to me; first, I don't believe in these abstract things called moral laws and I'm not too religious, so I don't believe in the law of God; you have to get a little more concrete, and more practical. What do you mean when you say that a law is unjust, and a law is just? Well, I would go on to say in more concrete terms that an unjust law is a code that the majority inflicts on the minority that is not binding on itself. So that this becomes difference made legal. Another thing that we can say is that an unjust law is a code which the majority inflicts upon the minority, which that minority had no part in enacting or creating, because that minority had no right to vote in many instances, so that the legislative bodies that made these laws were not democratically elected. Who could ever say that the legistative body of Mississippi was democratically elected, or the legislative body of Alabama was democratically elected, or the legislative body even of Georgia has been democratically elected, when there are people in Terrell County and in other counties because of the color of their skin who cannot vote? They confront reprisals and threats and all of that; so that an unjust law is a law that individuals did not have a part in creating or enacting because they were denied the right to vote.

Now the same token of just law would be just the opposite. A just law becomes saneness made legal. It is a code that the majority, who happen to believe in that code, compel the minority, who don't believe in it, to follow, because they are willing to follow it themselves, so it is saneness made legal. Therefore the individuals who stand up on the basis of civil disobedience realize that they are following something that says that there are just laws and there are unjust laws. Now, they are not anarchists. They believe that there are laws which must be followed; they do not seek to defy the law, they do not seek to evade the law. For many individuals who would call themselves segregationists and who would hold on to segregation at any cost seek to defy the law, they seek to evade the law, and their process can lead on into anarchy. They seek in the final analysis to follow a way of uncivil disobedience, not civil disobedience. And I submit that the individual who disobeys the law, whose conscience tells him it is unjust and who is willing to accept the penalty by staying in jail until that law is altered, is expressing at the moment the very highest respect for law.

This is what the students have followed in their movement. Of course there is nothing new about this; they feel that they are in good company and rightly so. We go back and read the Apology and the Crito, and you see Socrates practicing civil disobedience. And to a degree academic freedom is a reality today because Socrates practiced civil disobedience. The early Christians practiced civil disobedience in a superb manner, to a point where they were willing to be thrown to the lions. They were willing to face all kinds of suffering in order to stand up for what they knew was right even though they knew it was against the laws of the Roman Empire.

We could come up to our own day and we see it in many instances. We must never forget that everything that Hitler did in Germany was "legal." It was illegal to aid and comfort a Jew, in the days of Hitler's Germany. But I believe that if I had the same attitude then as I have now I would publicly aid and comfort my Jewish brothers in Germany if Hitler were alive today calling this an illegal process. If I lived in South Africa today in the midst of the white supremacy law in South Africa, I would join Chief Luthuli and others in saying break these unjust laws. And even let us come up to America. Our nation in a sense came into being through a massive act of civil disobedience for the Boston Tea Party was nothing but a massive act of civil disobedience. Those who stood up against the slave laws, the abolitionists, by and large practiced civil disobedience. So I think these students are in good company, and they feel that by practicing civil disobedience they are in line with men and women through the ages who have stood up for something that is morally right.

Now there are one or two other things that I want to say about this student movement, moving out of the philosophy of nonviolence, something about what it is a revolt against. On the one hand it is a revolt against the negative peace that has encompassed the South for many years. I remember when I was in Montgomery, Alabama, one of the white citizens came to me one day and said—and I think he was very sincere about this—that in Montgomery for all of these years we have been such a peaceful community, we have had so much harmony in race relations and then you people have started this movement and boycott, and it has done so much to disturb race relations, and we just don't love the Negro like we used to love them, because you have destroyed the harmony and the peace that we once had in race relations. And I said to him, in the best way I could say and I tried to say it in nonviolent terms, we have never had peace in Montgomery, Alabama, we have never had peace in the South. We have had a negative peace, which is merely the absence of tension; we've had a negative peace in which the Negro patiently accepted his situation and his plight, but we've never had true peace, we've never had positive peace, and what we're seeking now is to develop this positive peace. For we must come to see that peace is not merely the absence of some negative force, it is the presence of a positive force. True peace is not merely the absence of tension, but it is the presence of justice and brotherhood. I think this is what Jesus meant when he said, "I come not to bring peace but a sword." Now Jesus didn't mean he came to start war, to bring a physical sword, and he didn't mean, I come not to bring positive peace. But I think what Jesus was saying in substance was this, that I come not to bring an old negative peace, which makes for stagnant passivity and deadening complacency, I come to bring something different, and whenever I come, a conflict is precipitated, between the old and the new, whenever I come a struggle takes place between justice and injustice, between the forces of light and the forces of darkness. I come not to bring a negative peace, but a positive peace, which is brotherhood, which is justice, which is the Kingdom of God.

And I think this is what we are seeking to do today, and this movement is a revolt against a negative peace and a struggle to bring into being a positive peace, which makes for true brotherhood, true integration, true person-to-person relationships. This movement is also revolt against what is often called tokenism. Here again many people do not understand this, they feel that in this struggle the Negro will be satisfied with tokens of integration, just a few students and a few schools here and there and a few doors open here and there. But this isn't the meaning of the movement and I think that honesty impels me to admit it everywhere I have an opportunity, that the Negro's aim is to bring about complete integration in American life. And he has come to see that token integration is little more than token democracy, which ends up with many new evasive schemes and it ends up with new discrimination, covered up with such niceties of complexity. It is very interesting to discover that the movement has thrived in many communities that had token integration. So this reveals that the movement is based on a principle that integration must become real and complete, not just token integration.

It is also a revolt against what I often call the myth of time. We hear this quite often, that only time can solve this problem. That if we will only be patient, and only pray—which we must do, we must be patient and we must pray—but there are those who say just do these things and wait for time, and time will solve the problem. Well the people who argue this do not themselves realize that time is neutral, that it can be used constructively or destructively. At points the people of ill will, the segregationists, have used time much more effectively than the people of good will. So individuals in the struggle must come to realize that it is necessary to aid time, that without this kind of aid, time itself will become an ally of the insurgent and primitive forces of social stagnation. Therefore, this movement is a revolt against the myth of time.

There is a final thing that I would like to say to you, this movement is a movement based on faith in the future. It is a movement based on a philosophy, the possibility of the future bringing into being something real and meaningful. It is a movement based on hope. I think this is very important. The students have developed a theme song for their movement, maybe you've heard it. It goes something like this, "We shall overcome, deep in my heart, I do believe, we shall overcome," and then they go on to say another verse, "We are not afraid, we are not afraid today, deep in my heart I do believe, we shall overcome." So it is out of this deep faith in the future that they are able to move out and adjourn the councils of despair, and to bring new light in the dark chambers of pessimism. I can remember the times that we've been together, I remember that night in Montgomery, Alabama, when we had stayed up all night discussing the Freedom Rides, and that morning came to see that it was necessary to go on with the Freedom Rides, that we would not in all good conscience call an end to the Freedom Rides at that point. And I remember the first group got ready to leave, to take a bus for Jackson, Mississippi, we all joined hands and started singing together. "We shall overcome, we shall overcome." And something within me said, now how is it that these students can sing this, they are going down to Mississippi, they are going to face hostile and jeering mobs, and yet they could sing, "We shall overcome." They may even face physical death, and yet they could sing, "We shall overcome." Most of them realized that they would be thrown into jail, and yet they could sing, "We shall overcome, we are not afraid." Then something caused me to see at that moment the real meaning of the movement. That students had faith in the future. That the movement was based on hope, that this movement had something within it that says somehow even though the arc of the moral universe is long, it bends toward justice. And I think this should be a challenge to all others who are struggling to transform the dangling discords of our Southland into a beautiful symphony of brotherhood. There is something in this student movement which says to us, that we shall overcome. Before the victory is won some may have to get scarred up, but we shall overcome. Before the victory of brotherhood is achieved, some will maybe face physical death, but we shall overcome. Before the victory is won, some will lose jobs, some will be called communists, and reds, merely because they believe in brotherhood, some will be dismissed as dangerous rabblerousers and agitators merely because they're standing up for what is right, but we shall overcome. That is the basis of this movement, and as I like to say, there is something in this universe that justifies Carlyle in saying no lie can live forever. We shall overcome because there is something in this universe which justifies William Cullen Bryant in saying truth crushed to earth shall rise again. We shall overcome because there is something in this universe that justifies James Russell Lowell in saying, truth forever on the scaffold, wrong forever on the throne. Yet that scaffold sways the future, and behind the dim unknown standeth God within the shadows keeping watch above His own. With this faith in the future, with this determined struggle, we will be able to emerge from the bleak and desolate midnight of man's inhumanity to man, into the bright and glittering daybreak of freedom and justice. Thank you.

MARTIN LUTHER KING, JR.

Letter from Birmingham City Jail (1963)

The immediacy of this essay has made it, after Thoreau's "Civil Disobedience," the most famous and greatest of American writings on civil disobedience. Dr. King explains: "In any nonviolent campaign there are four basic steps: (1) collection of the facts to determine whether injustices are alive, (2) negotiation, (3) self-purification, and (4) direct action. We have gone through all of these steps in Birmingham. There can be no gainsaying of the fact that racial injustice engulfs this community." In 1967, the year before he was assassinated, he spoke in the lecture "Conscience for Change" about the power of civil disobedience: "Mass civil disobedience as a new stage of struggle can transmute the deep rage of the ghetto into a constructive and creative force. To dislocate the functioning of a city without destroying it can be more effective than a riot because it can be longer lasting, costly to the larger society, but not wantonly destructive. Finally, it is a device of social action that is more difficult for the government to quell by superior force."[1]

MY DEAR FELLOW Clergymen,

While confined here in the Birmingham city jail, I came across your recent statement calling our present activities "unwise and untimely." Seldom, if ever, do I pause to answer criticism of my work and ideas. If I sought to answer all of the criticisms that cross my desk, my secretaries would be engaged in little else in the course of the day, and I would have no time for constructive work. But since I feel that you are men of genuine good will and your criticisms are sincerely set forth, I would like to answer your statement in what I hope will be patient and reasonable terms.

I think I should give the reason for my being in Birmingham, since you have been influenced by the argument of "outsiders

---

[1] *The Lost Massey Lectures: Recovered Classics from Five Great Thinkers.* Toronto: House of Anansi Press. 2007. 174.

coming in." I have the honor of serving as president of the Southern Christian Leadership Conference, an organization operating in every southern state, with headquarters in Atlanta, Georgia. We have some eighty-five affiliate organizations all across the South—one being the Alabama Christian Movement for Human Rights. Whenever necessary and possible we share staff, educational and financial resources with our affiliates. Several months ago our local affiliate here in Birmingham invited us to be on call to engage in a nonviolent direct-action program if such were deemed necessary. We readily consented and when the hour came we lived up to our promises. So I am here, along with several members of my staff, because we were invited here. I am here because I have basic organizational ties here.

Beyond this, I am in Birmingham because injustice is here. Just as the eighth century prophets left their little villages and carried their "thus saith the Lord" far beyond the boundaries of their hometowns; and just as the Apostle Paul left his little village of Tarsus and carried the gospel of Jesus Christ to practically every hamlet and city of the Graeco-Roman world, I too am compelled to carry the gospel of freedom beyond my particular hometown. Like Paul, I must constantly respond to the Macedonian call for aid.

Moreover, I am cognizant of the interrelatedness of all communities and states. I cannot sit idly by in Atlanta and not be concerned about what happens in Birmingham. Injustice anywhere is a threat to justice everywhere. We are caught in an inescapable network of mutuality, tied in a single garment of destiny. Whatever affects one directly affects all indirectly. Never again can we afford to live with the narrow, provincial "outside agitator" idea. Anyone who lives in the United States can never be considered an outsider anywhere in this country.

You deplore the demonstrations that are presently taking place in Birmingham. But I am sorry that your statement did not express a similar concern for the conditions that brought the demonstrations into being. I am sure that each of you would want to go beyond the superficial social analyst who looks merely at effects, and does not grapple with underlying causes. I would not hesitate to say that it is unfortunate that so-called demonstrations are taking place in Birmingham at this time, but I would say in more emphatic terms that it is even more unfortunate that the white power structure of this city left the Negro community with no other alternative.

In any nonviolent campaign there are four basic steps: (1) collection of the facts to determine whether injustices are alive, (2) negotiation,

(3) self-purification, and (4) direct action. We have gone through all of these steps in Birmingham. There can be no gainsaying of the fact that racial injustice engulfs this community.

Birmingham is probably the most thoroughly segregated city in the United States. Its ugly record of police brutality is known in every section of this country. Its injust treatment of Negroes in the courts is a notorious reality. There have been more unsolved bombings of Negro homes and churches in Birmingham than any city in this nation. These are the hard, brutal and unbelievable facts. On the basis of these conditions Negro leaders sought to negotiate with the city fathers. But the political leaders consistently refused to engage in good faith negotiation.

Then came the opportunity last September to talk with some of the leaders of the economic community. In these negotiating sessions certain promises were made by the merchants—such as the promise to remove the humiliating racial signs from the stores. On the basis of these promises Rev. Shuttlesworth and the leaders of the Alabama Christian Movement for Human Rights agreed to call a moratorium on any type of demonstrations. As the weeks and months unfolded we realized that we were the victims of a broken promise. The signs remained. Like so many experiences of the past we were confronted with blasted hopes, and the dark shadow of a deep disappointment settled upon us. So we had no alternative except that of preparing for direct action, whereby we would present our very bodies as a means of laying our case before the conscience of the local and national community. We were not unmindful of the difficulties involved. So we decided to go through a process of self-purification. We started having workshops on nonviolence and repeatedly asked ourselves the questions, "Are you able to accept without retaliating?" "Are you able to endure the ordeals of jail?" We decided to set our direct-action program around the Easter season, realizing that with the exception of Christmas, this was the largest shopping period of the year. Knowing that a strong economic withdrawal program would be the by-product of direct action, we felt that this was best time to bring pressure on the merchants for the needed changes. Then it occurred to us that the March election was ahead and we speedily decided to postpone action until after election day. When we discovered that Mr. Connor was in the run-off, we decided again to postpone action so that the demonstrations could not be used to cloud the issues. At this time we agreed to begin our nonviolent witness the day after the run-off.

This reveals that we did not move irresponsibly into direct action. We too wanted to see Mr. Connor defeated; so we went through postponement after postponement to aid in this community need. After this we felt that direct action could be delayed no longer.

You may well ask, "Why direct action? Why sit-ins, marches, etc.? Isn't negotiation a better path?" You are exactly right in your call for negotiation. Indeed, this is the purpose of direct action. Nonviolent direct action seeks to create such a crisis and establish such creative tension that a community that has constantly refused to negotiate is forced to confront the issue. It seeks so to dramatize the issue that it can no longer be ignored. I just referred to the creation of tension as a part of the work of the nonviolent resister. This may sound rather shocking. But I must confess that I am not afraid of the word tension. I have earnestly worked and preached against violent tension, but there is a type of constructive nonviolent tension that is necessary for growth. Just as Socrates felt that it was necessary to create a tension in the mind so that individuals could rise from the bondage of myths and half-truths to the unfettered realm of creative analysis and objective appraisal, we must see the need of having nonviolent gadflies to create the kind of tension in society that will help men to rise from the dark depths of prejudice and racism to the majestic heights of understanding and brotherhood. So the purpose of the direct action is to create a situation so crisis-packed that it will inevitably open the door to negotiation. We, therefore, concur with you in your call for negotiation. Too long has our beloved Southland been bogged down in the tragic attempt to live in monologue rather than dialogue.

One of the basic points in your statement is that our acts are untimely. Some have asked, "Why didn't you give the new administration time to act?" The only answer that I can give to this inquiry is that the new administration must be prodded about as much as the outgoing one before it acts. We will be sadly mistaken if we feel that the election of Mr. Boutwell will bring the millennium to Birmingham. While Mr. Boutwell is much more articulate and gentle than Mr. Connor, they are both segregationists, dedicated to the task of maintaining the status quo. The hope I see in Mr. Boutwell is that he will be reasonable enough to see the futility of massive resistance to desegregation. But he will not see this without pressure from the devotees of civil rights. My friends, I must say to you that we have not made a single gain in civil rights without determined legal and nonviolent pressure. History is the long and tragic story of the fact that privileged groups seldom give up their privileges voluntarily. Individuals may see the moral light and voluntarily give up their unjust posture; but as Reinhold Niebuhr has reminded us, groups are more immoral than individuals.

We know through painful experience that freedom is never voluntarily given by the oppressor; it must be demanded by the oppressed. Frankly, I have never yet engaged in a direct action movement that was "well-timed," according to the timetable of those who have not suffered unduly from the disease of segregation. For years now I have heard the words "Wait!" It rings in the ear of every Negro with a piercing familiarity. This "Wait" has almost always meant "Never." It has been a tranquilizing thalidomide, relieving the emotional stress for a moment, only to give birth to an ill-formed infant of frustration. We must come to see with the distinguished jurist of yesterday that "justice too long delayed is justice denied." We have waited for more than 340 years for our constitutional and God-given rights. The nations of Asia and Africa are moving with jetlike speed toward the goal of political independence, and we still creep at horse and buggy pace toward the gaining of a cup of coffee at a lunch counter. I guess it is easy for those who have never felt the stinging darts of segregation to say, "Wait." But when you have seen vicious mobs lynch your mothers and fathers at will and drown your sisters and brothers at whim; when you have seen hate-filled policemen curse, kick, brutalize and even kill your black brothers and sisters with impunity; when you see the vast majority of your twenty million Negro brothers smothering in an airtight cage of poverty in the midst of an affluent society; when you suddenly find your tongue twisted and your speech stammering as you seek to explain to your six-year-old daughter why she can't go to the public amusement park that has just been advertised on television, and see tears welling up in her little eyes when she is told that Funtown is closed to colored children, and see the depressing clouds of inferiority begin to form in her little mental sky, and see her begin to distort her little personality by unconsciously developing a bitterness toward white people; when you have to concoct an answer for a five-year-old son asking in agonizing pathos: "Daddy, why do white people treat colored people so mean?"; when you take a cross-country drive and find it necessary to sleep night after night in the uncomfortable corners of your automobile because no motel will accept you; when you are humiliated day in and day out by nagging signs reading "white" and "colored"; when your first name becomes "nigger" and your middle name becomes "boy" (however old you are) and your last name becomes "John," and when your wife and mother are never given the respected title "Mrs."; when you are harried by day and haunted by night by the fact that you are a Negro, living constantly at tiptoe stance never quite knowing what to expect next, and plagued with inner fears and outer resentments; when you are forever fighting a degenerating sense of "nobodiness"; then you will understand why we find it difficult to wait. There comes a time when the cup of endurance runs over, and men are no longer willing to be plunged into an abyss of injustice where they experience the blackness of corroding despair. I hope, sirs, you can understand our legitimate and unavoidable impatience.

You express a great deal of anxiety over our willingness to break laws. This is certainly a legitimate concern. Since we so diligently urge people to obey the Supreme Court's decision of 1954 outlawing segregation in the public schools, it is rather strange and paradoxical to find us consciously breaking laws. One may well ask, "How can you advocate breaking some laws and obeying others?" The answer is found in the fact that there are two types of laws: there are *just* and there are *unjust* laws. I would agree with Saint Augustine that "An unjust law is no law at all."

Now what is the difference between the two? How does one determine when a law is just or unjust? A just law is a man-made code that squares with the moral law or the law of God. An unjust law is a code that is out of harmony with the moral law. To put it in the terms of Saint Thomas Aquinas, an unjust law is a human law that is not rooted in eternal and natural law. Any law that uplifts human personality is just. Any law that degrades human personality is unjust. All segregation statutes are unjust because segregation distorts the soul and damages the personality. It gives the segregator a false sense of superiority, and the segregated a false sense of inferiority. To use the words of Martin Buber, the great Jewish philosopher, segregation substitutes an "I-it" relationship for the "I-thou" relationship, and ends up relegating persons to the status of things. So segregation is not only politically, economically and sociologically unsound, but it is morally wrong and sinful. Paul Tillich has said that sin is separation. Isn't segregation an existential expression of man's tragic separation, an expression of his awful

estrangement, his terrible sinfulness? So I can urge men to disobey
segregation ordinances because they are morally wrong.

Let us turn to a more concrete example of just and unjust laws.
An unjust law is a code that a majority inflicts on a minority that is
not binding on itself. This is difference made legal. On the other
hand a just law is a code that a majority compels a minority to follow that it is willing to follow itself. This is sameness made legal.

Let me give another explanation. An unjust law is a code
inflicted upon a minority which that minority had no part in enacting or creating because they did not have the unhampered right to
vote. Who can say that the legislature of Alabama which set up the
segregation laws was democratically elected? Throughout the state
of Alabama all types of conniving methods are used to prevent
Negroes from becoming registered voters and there are some counties without a single Negro registered to vote despite the fact that
the Negro constitutes a majority of the population. Can any law set
up in such a state be considered democratically structured?

These are just a few examples of unjust and just laws. There are
some instances when a law is just on its face and unjust in its application. For instance, I was arrested Friday on a change of parading
without a permit. Now there is nothing wrong with an ordinance
which requires a permit for a parade, but when the ordinance is
used to preserve segregation and to deny citizens the First
Amendment privilege of peaceful assembly and peaceful protest,
then it becomes unjust.

I hope you can see the distinction I am trying to point out. In
no sense do I advocate evading or defying the law as the rabid seg-
regationist would do. This would lead to anarchy. One who breaks
an unjust law must do it *openly, lovingly* (not hatefully as the white
mothers did in New Orleans when they were seen on television
screaming, "nigger, nigger, nigger"), and with a willingness to
accept the penalty. I submit that an individual who breaks a law that
conscience tells him is unjust, and willingly accepts the penalty by
staying in jail to arouse the conscience of the community over its
injustice, is in reality expressing the very highest respect for law.

Of course, there is nothing new about this kind of civil disobedience. It was seen sublimely in the refusal of Shadrach, Meshach and
Abednego to obey the laws of Nebuchadnezzar because a higher
moral law was involved. It was practiced superbly by the early
Christians who were willing to face hungry lions and the excruciat-
ing pain of chopping blocks, before submitting to certain unjust

laws of the Roman Empire. To a degree academic freedom is a reality today because Socrates practiced civil disobedience.

We can never forget that everything Hitler did in Germany was "legal" and everything the Hungarian freedom fighters did in Hungary was "illegal." It was "illegal" to aid and comfort a Jew in Hitler's Germany. But I am sure that if I had lived in Germany during that time I would have aided and comforted my Jewish brothers even though it was illegal. If I lived in a Communist country today where certain principles dear to the Christian faith are suppressed, I believe I would openly advocate disobeying these anti-religious laws. I must make two honest confessions to you, my Christian and Jewish brothers. First, I must confess that over the last few years I have been gravely disappointed with the white moderate. I have almost reached the regrettable conclusion that the Negro's great stumbling block in the stride toward freedom is not the White Citizen's Counciler or the Ku Klux Klanner, but the white moderate who is more devoted to "order" than to justice; who prefers a negative peace which is the absence of tension to a positive peace which is the presence of justice; who constantly says, "I agree with you in the goal you seek, but I can't agree with your methods of direct action"; who paternalistically feels that he can set the timetable for another man's freedom; who lives by the myth of time and who constantly advised the Negro to wait until a "more convenient season." Shallow understanding from people of good will is more frustrating than absolute misunderstanding from people of ill will. Lukewarm acceptance is much more bewildering than outright rejection.

I had hoped that the white moderate would understand that law and order exist for the purpose of establishing justice, and that when they fail to do this they become dangerously structured dams that block the flow of social progress. I had hoped that the white moderate would understand that the present tension of the South is merely a necessary phase of the transition from an obnoxious negative peace, where the Negro passively accepted his unjust plight, to a substance-filled positive peace, where all men will respect the dignity and worth of human personality. Actually, we who engage in nonviolent direct action are not the creators of tension. We merely bring to the surface the hidden tension that is already alive. We bring it out in the open where it can be seen and dealt with. Like a boil that can never be cured as long as it is covered up but must be opened with all its pus-flowing ugliness to the natural medicines of air and light, injustice must likewise be exposed, with all of the tension its exposing creates, to the light of human conscience and the air of national opinion before it can be cured.

In your statement you asserted that our actions, even though peaceful, must be condemned because they precipitate violence. But can this assertion be logically made? Isn't this like condemning the robbed man because his possession of money precipitated the evil act of robbery? Isn't this like condemning Socrates because his unswerving commitment to truth and his philosophical delvings precipitated the misguided popular mind to make him drink the hemlock? Isn't this like condemning Jesus because His unique God-consciousness and never-ceasing devotion to his will precipitated the evil act of crucifixion? We must come to see, as federal courts have consistently affirmed, that it is immoral to urge an individual to withdraw his efforts to gain his basic constitutional rights because the quest precipitates violence. Society must protect the robbed and punish the robber.

I had also hoped that the white moderate would reject the myth of time. I received a letter this morning from a white brother in Texas which said: "All Christians know that the colored people will receive equal rights eventually, but it is possible that you are in too great of a religious hurry. It has taken Christianity almost two thousand years to accomplish what it has. The teachings of Christ take time to come to earth." All that is said here grows out of a tragic misconception of time. It is the strangely irrational notion that there is something in the very flow of time that will inevitably cure all ills. Actually time is neutral. It can be used either destructively or constructively. I am coming to feel that the people of ill will have used time much more effectively than the people of good will. We will have to repent in this generation not merely for the vitriolic words and actions of the bad people, but for the appalling silence of the good people. We must come to see that human progress never rolls in on wheels of inevitability. It comes through the tireless efforts and persistent work of men willing to be co-workers with God, and without this hard work time itself becomes an ally of the forces of social stagnation. We must use time creatively, and forever realize that the time is always ripe to do right. Now is the time to make real the promise of democracy, and transform our pending national elegy into a creative psalm of brotherhood. Now is the time to lift our national policy from the quicksand of racial injustice to the solid rock of human dignity.

You spoke of our activity in Birmingham as extreme. At first I was rather disappointed that fellow clergymen would see my non-violent efforts as those of the extremist. I started thinking about the fact that I stand in the middle of two opposing forces in the Negro community. One is a force of complacency made up of Negroes who, as a result of long years of oppression, have been so completely drained of self-respect and a sense of "somebodiness" that they have adjusted to segregation, and, of a few Negroes in the middle class who, because of a degree of academic and economic security, and because at points they profit by segregation, have unconsciously become insensitive to the problems of the masses. The other force is one of bitterness and hatred, and comes perilously close to advocating violence. It is expressed in the various black nationalist groups that are springing up over the nation, the largest and best known being Elijah Muhammad's Muslim movement. This movement is nourished by the contemporary frustration over the continued existence of racial discrimination. It is made up of people who have lost faith in America, who have absolutely repudiated Christianity, and who have concluded that the white man is an incurable "devil." I have tried to stand between these two forces, saying that we need not follow the "do-nothingism" of the complacent or the hatred and despair of the black nationalist. There is the more excellent way of love and nonviolent protest. I'm grateful to God that, through the Negro church, the dimension of non-violence entered our struggle. If this philosophy had not emerged, I am convinced that by now many streets of the South would be flowing with floods of blood. And I am further convinced that if our white brothers dismiss us as "rabble-rousers" and "outside agitators" those of us who are working through the channels of non-violent direct action and refuse to support our nonviolent efforts, millions of Negroes, out of frustration and despair, will seek solace and security in black nationalist ideologies, a development that will lead inevitably to a frightening racial nightmare.

Oppressed people cannot remain oppressed forever. The urge for freedom will eventually come. This is what happened to the American Negro. Something within has reminded him of his birthright of freedom; something without has reminded him that he can gain it. Consciously and unconsciously, he has been swept in by what the Germans call the *Zeitgeist,* and with his black brothers of Africa, and his brown and yellow brothers of Asia, South America and the Caribbean, he is moving with a sense of cosmic urgency toward the promised land of racial justice. Recognizing this vital urge that has engulfed the Negro community, one should readily understand public demonstrations. The Negro has many pent-up resentments and latent frustrations. He has to get them out. So let him march sometime; let him have his prayer pilgrimages to the city hall; understand why he must have sit-ins and freedom rides. If his repressed emotions do not come out in these nonviolent ways, they will come out in ominous expressions of violence. This is not a threat; it is a fact of history. So I have not said to my people "get rid of your discontent." But I have tried to say that this normal and healthy discontent can be channelized through the creative outlet of nonviolent direct action. Now this approach is being dismissed as extremist. I must admit that I was initially disappointed in being so categorized.

But as I continued to think about the matter I gradually gained a bit of satisfaction from being considered an extremist. Was not Jesus an extremist in love—"Love your enemies, bless them that curse you, pray for them that despitefully use you." Was not Amos an extremist for justice—"Let justice roll down like waters and righteousness like a mighty stream." Was not Paul an extremist for the gospel of Jesus Christ—"I bear in my body the marks of the Lord Jesus." Was not Martin Luther an extremist—"Here I stand; I can do none other so help me God." Was not John Bunyan an extremist—"I will stay in jail to the end of my days before I make a butchery of my conscience." Was not Abraham Lincoln an extremist—"This nation cannot survive half slave and half free." Was not Thomas Jefferson an extremist—"We hold these truths to be self-evident, that all men are created equal." So the question is not whether we will be extremist but what kind of extremist will we be. Will we be extremists for hate or will we be extremists for love? Will we be extremists for the preservation of injustice—or will we be extremists for the cause of justice? In that dramatic scene on Calvary's hill, three men were crucified. We must not forget that all three were crucified for the same crime—the crime of extremism. Two were extremists for immorality, and thusly fell below their environment. The other, Jesus Christ, was an extremist for love, truth and goodness, and thereby rose above his environment. So, after all, maybe the South, the nation and the world are in dire need of creative extremists.

I had hoped that the white moderate would see this. Maybe I was too optimistic. Maybe I expected too much. I guess I should have realized that few members of a race that has oppressed another race can understand or appreciate the deep groans and passionate yearnings of those that have been oppressed and still fewer have the vision to see that injustice must be rooted out by strong, persistent and determined action. I am thankful, however, that some of our white brothers have grasped the meaning of this social revolution and committed themselves to it. They are still all too small in quantity, but they are big in quality. Some like Ralph McGill, Lillian Smith, Harry Golden and James Dabbs have written about our struggle in eloquent, prophetic and understanding terms. Others have marched with us down nameless streets of the South. They have languished in filthy roach-infested jails, suffering the abuse and brutality of angry policemen who see them as "dirty nigger-lovers." They, unlike so many of their moderate brothers and sisters, have recognized the urgency of the moment and sensed the need for powerful "action" antidotes to combat the disease of segregation.

Let me rush on to mention my other disappointment. I have been so greatly disappointed with the white church and its leadership. Of course, there are some notable exceptions. I am not unmindful of the fact that each of you has taken some significant stands on this issue. I commend you, Rev. Stallings, for your Christian stance on this past Sunday, in welcoming Negroes to your worship service on a non-segregated basis. I commend the Catholic leaders of this state for integrating Springhill College several years ago.

But despite these notable exceptions I must honestly reiterate that I have been disappointed with the church. I do not say that as one of the negative critics who can always find something wrong with the church. I say it as a minister of the gospel, who loves the church; who was nurtured in its bosom; who has been sustained by its spiritual blessings and who will remain true to it as long as the cord of life shall lengthen.

I had the strange feeling when I was suddenly catapulted into the leadership of the bus protest in Montgomery several years ago that we would have the support of the white church. I felt that the white ministers, priests and rabbis of the South would be some of our strongest allies. Instead, some have been outright opponents, refusing to understand the freedom movement and misrepresenting its leaders; all too many others have been more cautious than courageous and have remained silent behind the anesthetizing security of the stained-glass windows.

In spite of my shattered dreams of the past, I came to Birmingham with the hope that the white religious leadership of this community would see the justice of our cause, and with deep moral concern, serve as the channel through which our just grievances would get to the power structure. I had hoped that each of you would understand. But again I have been disappointed. I have heard numerous religious leaders of the South call upon their worshippers to comply with a desegregation decision because it is the *law,* but I have longed to hear white ministers say, "Follow this decree because integration is morally *right* and the Negro is your brother." In the midst of blatant injustices inflicted upon the Negro, I have watched white churches stand on the sideline and merely mouth pious irrelevancies and sanctimonious trivialities. In the midst of a mighty struggle to rid our nation of racial and economic injustice, I have heard so many ministers say, "Those are social issues with which the gospel has no real concern," and I have watched so many churches commit themselves to a completely otherworldly religion which made a strange distinction between body and soul, the sacred and the secular.

So here we are moving toward the exit of the twentieth century with a religious community largely adjusted to the status quo, standing as a taillight behind other community agencies rather than a headlight leading men to higher levels of justice.

I have traveled the length and breadth of Alabama, Mississippi and all the other southern states. On sweltering summer days and crisp autumn mornings I have looked at her beautiful churches with their lofty spires pointing heavenward. I have beheld the impressive outlay of her massive religious education buildings. Over and over again I have found myself asking: "What kind of people worship here? Who is their God? Where were their voices when the lips of Governor Barnett dripped with words of interposition and nullification? Where were they when Governor Wallace gave the clarion call for defiance and hatred? Where were their voices of support when tired, bruised and weary Negro men and women decided to rise from the dark dungeons of complacency to the bright hills of creative protest?"

Yes, these questions are still in my mind. In deep disappointment, I have wept over the laxity of the church. But be assured that my tears have been tears of love. There can be no deep disappointment where there is not deep love. Yes, I love the church; I love her sacred walls. How could I do otherwise? I am in the rather unique position of being the son, the grandson and the great-grandson of preachers. Yes, I see the church as the body of Christ. But, oh! How we have blemished and scarred that body through social neglect and fear of being nonconformists.

There was a time when the church was very powerful. It was during that period when the early Christians rejoiced when they were deemed worthy to suffer for what they believed. In those days the church was not merely a thermometer that recorded the ideas and principles of popular opinion; it was a thermostat that transformed the mores of society. Wherever the early Christians entered a town the power structure got disturbed and immediately sought to convict them for being "disturbers of the peace" and "outside agitators." But they went on with the conviction that they were "a colony of heaven," and had to obey God rather than man. They were small in number but big in commitment. They were too God-intoxicated to be "astronomically intimidated." They brought an end to such ancient evils as infanticide and gladiatorial contest.

Things are different now. The contemporary church is often a weak, ineffectual voice with an uncertain sound. It is so often the arch-supporter of the status quo. Far from being disturbed by the presence of the church, the power structure of the average community is consoled by the church's silent and often vocal sanction of things as they are.

But the judgment of God is upon the church as never before. If the church of today does not recapture the sacrificial spirit of the early church, it will lose its authentic ring, forfeit the loyalty of millions, and be dismissed as an irrelevant social club with no meaning for the twentieth century. I am meeting young people every day whose disappointment with the church has risen to outright disgust.

Maybe again, I have been too optimistic. Is organized religion too inextricably bound to the status quo to save our nation and the world? Maybe I must turn my faith to the inner spiritual church, the church within the church, as the true *ecclesia* and the hope of the world. But again I am thankful to God that some noble souls from the ranks of organized religion have broken loose from the paralyzing chains of conformity and joined us as active partners in the struggle for freedom. They have left their secure congregations and walked the streets of Albany, Georgia, with us. They have gone through the highways of the South on tortuous rides for freedom. Yes, they have gone to jail with us. Some have been kicked out of their churches, and lost support of their bishops and fellow ministers. But they have gone with the faith that right defeated is stronger than evil triumphant. These men have been the leaven in the lump of the race. Their witness has been the spiritual salt that has preserved the true meaning of the gospel in these troubled times. They have carved a tunnel of hope through the dark mountain of disappointment.

I hope the church as a whole will meet the challenge of this decisive hour. But even if the church does not come to the aid of justice, I have no despair about the future. I have no fear about the outcome of our struggle in Birmingham, even if our motives are presently misunderstood. We will reach the goal of freedom in Birmingham and all over the nation, because the goal of America is freedom. Abused and scorned though we may be, our destiny is tied up with the destiny of America. Before the Pilgrims landed at Plymouth we were here. Before the pen of Jefferson etched across the pages of history the majestic words of the Declaration of Independence, we were here. For more than two centuries our foreparents labored in this country without wages; they made cotton king; and they built the homes of their masters in the midst of brutal injustice and shameful humiliation—and yet out of a bottomless vitality they continued to thrive and develop. If the inexpressible cruelties of slavery could not stop us, the opposition we now face will surely fail. We will win our freedom because the sacred heritage of our nation and the eternal will of God are embodied in our echoing demands.

I must close now. But before closing I am impelled to mention one other point in your statement that troubled me profoundly. You warmly commended the Birmingham police force for keeping "order" and "preventing violence." I don't believe you would have so warmly commended the police force if you had seen its angry violent dogs literally biting six unarmed, nonviolent Negroes. I don't believe you would so quickly commend the policemen if you would observe their ugly and inhuman treatment of Negroes here in the city jail; if you would watch them push and curse old Negro women and young Negro girls; if you would see them slap and kick old Negro men and young boys; if you will observe them, as they did on two occasions, refuse to give us food because we wanted to sing our grace together. I'm sorry that I can't join you in your praise for the police department.

It is true that they have been rather disciplined in their public handling of the demonstrators. In this sense they have been rather publicly "nonviolent." But for what purpose? To preserve the evil system of segregation. Over the last few years I have consistently preached that nonviolence demands that the means we use must be as pure as the ends we seek. So I have tried to make it clear that it is wrong to use immoral means to attain moral ends. But now I must affirm that it is just as wrong, or even more so, to use moral means to preserve immoral ends. Maybe Mr. Connor and his policemen have been rather publicly nonviolent, as Chief Pritchett was in Albany, Georgia, but they have used the moral means of nonviolence to maintain the immoral end of flagrant racial injustice. T. S. Eliot has said that there is no greater treason than to do the right deed for the wrong reason.

I wish you had commended the Negro sit-inners and demonstrators of Birmingham for their sublime courage, their willingness to suffer and their amazing discipline in the midst of the most inhuman provocation.

One day the South will recognize its real heroes. They will be the James Merediths, courageously and with a majestic sense of purpose facing jeering and hostile mobs and the agonizing loneliness that characterizes the life of the pioneer. They will be old, oppressed, battered Negro women, symbolized in a seventy-two-year-old woman of Montgomery, Alabama, who rose up with a sense of dignity and with her people decided not to ride the segregated buses, and responded to one who inquired about her tiredness with ungrammatical profundity: "My feet is tired, but my soul is rested." They will be the young high school and college students, young ministers of the gospel and a host of their elders courageously and nonviolently sitting-in at lunch counters and willingly going to jail for conscience's sake. One day the South will know that when these disinherited children of God sat down at lunch counters they were in reality standing up for the best in the American dream and the most sacred values in our Judeo-Christian heritage, and thusly, carrying our whole nation back to those great wells of democracy which were dug deep by the Founding Fathers in the formulation of the Constitution and the Declaration of Independence.

Never before have I written a letter this long (or should I say a book?). I'm afraid that it is much too long to take your precious time. I can assure you that it would have been much shorter if I had been writing from a comfortable desk, but what else is there to do when you are alone for days in the dull monotony of a narrow jail cell other than write long letters, think strange thoughts, and pray long prayers?

If I have said anything in this letter that is an overstatement of the truth and is indicative of an unreasonable impatience, I beg you to forgive me. If I have said anything in this letter that is an understatement of the truth and is indicative of my having a patience that makes me patient with anything less than brotherhood, I beg God to forgive me.

I hope this letter finds you strong in the faith. I also hope that circumstances will soon make it possible for me to meet each of you, not as an integrationist or a civil rights leader, but as a fellow clergyman and a Christian brother. Let us all hope that the dark clouds of racial prejudice will soon pass away and the deep fog of misunderstanding will be lifted from our fear-drenched communities and in some not too distant tomorrow the radiant stars of love and brotherhood will shine over our great nation with all of their scintillating beauty.

Yours for the cause of Peace and Brotherhood,

Martin Luther King, Jr.

BERTRAND RUSSELL

Civil Disobedience and the Threat of Nuclear Warfare (1963)

The famed British philosopher Bertrand Russell (1872–1970) had spoken out against warfare ever since World War I, and was fired from his post as a lecturer at Cambridge University as a result. The winner of the Nobel Prize for Literature in 1950, in 1958 he founded the Campaign for Nuclear Disarmament, and in 1963 established the Bertrand Russell Peace Foundation. While the nuclear war he feared has not happened, the world knows there have been instances where it was narrowly averted, like the missile crisis between the United States and the Soviet Union, to which Russell alludes.

THE COMMITTEE OF 100, as your readers are aware, calls for non-violent civil disobedience on a large scale as a means of inducing the British Government (and others, we hope, in due course) to abandon nuclear weapons and the protection that they are supposed to afford. Many critics have objected that civil disobedience is immoral, at any rate where the government is democratic. It is my purpose to combat this view, not in general, but in the case of non-violent civil disobedience on behalf of certain aims advocated by the Committee of 100.

It is necessary to begin with some abstract principles of ethics. There are, broadly speaking, two types of ethical theory. One of these, which is exemplified in the Decalogue, lays down rules of conduct which are supposed to hold in all cases, regardless of the effects of obeying them. The other theory, while admitting that some rules of conduct are valid in a very great majority of cases, is prepared to consider the consequences of actions and to permit breaches of the rules where the consequences of obeying the rules are obviously undesirable. In practice, most people adopt the second point of view, and only appeal to the first in controversies with opponents.

Let us take a few examples. Suppose a physically powerful man, suffering from hydrophobia, was about to bite your children, and the only way of preventing him was to kill him. I think very few people would think you unjustified in adopting this method of saving your children's lives. Those who thought you justified would not deny that the prohibition of murder is *almost* always right. Probably they would go on to say that this particular sort of killing should not be called "murder." They would define "murder" as "unjustifiable homicide." In that case, the precept that murder is wrong becomes a tautology, but the ethical question remains: "What sort of killing is to be labelled as murder?" Or take, again, the commandment not to steal. Almost everybody would agree that in an immense majority of cases it is right to obey this commandment. But suppose you were a refugee, fleeing with your family from persecution, and you could not obtain food except by stealing. Most people would agree that you would be justified in stealing. The only exceptions would be those who approved of the tyranny from which you were trying to escape.

There have been many cases in history where the issue was not so clear. In the time of Pope Gregory VI, simony was rife in the Church. Pope Gregory VI, by means of simony, became Pope and did so in order to abolish simony. In this he was largely successful, and final success was achieved by his disciple and admirer, Pope Gregory VII, who was one of the most illustrious of Popes. I will not express an opinion on the conduct of Gregory VI, which has remained a controversial issue down to the present day.

The only rule, in all such doubtful cases, is to consider the consequences of the action in question. We must include among these consequences the bad effect of weakening respect for a rule which is usually right. But, even when this is taken into account, there will be cases where even the most generally acceptable rule of conduct should be broken.

So much for general theory. I will come now one step nearer to the moral problem with which we are concerned.

What is to be said about a rule enjoining respect for law? Let us first consider the arguments in favour of such a rule. Without law, a civilized community is impossible. Where there is general disrespect for the law, all kinds of evil consequences are sure to follow. A notable example was the failure of prohibition in America. In this case it became obvious that the only cure was a change in the law, since it was impossible to obtain general respect for the law as it stood. This view prevailed, in spite of the fact that those who broke the law were not actuated by what are called conscientious motives. This case made it obvious that respect for the law has two sides. If there is to be respect for the law, the law must be generally considered to be worthy of respect.

The main argument in favour of respect for law is that, in disputes between two parties, it substitutes a neutral authority for private bias which would be likely in the absence of law. The force which the law can exert is, in most such cases, irresistible, and therefore only has to be invoked in the case of a minority of reckless criminals. The net result is a community in which most people are peaceful. These reasons for the reign of law are admitted in the great majority of cases, except by anarchists. I have no wish to dispute their validity save in exceptional circumstances.

There is one very large class of cases in which the law does not have the merit of being impartial as between the disputants. This is when one of the disputants is the state. The state makes the laws and, unless there is a very vigilant public opinion in defence of justifiable liberties, the state will make the law such as suits its own convenience, which may not be what is for the public good. In the Nuremberg trials war criminals were condemned for obeying the orders of the state, though their condemnation was only possible after the state in question had suffered military defeat. But it is noteworthy that the powers which defeated Germany all agreed that failure to practise civil disobedience may deserve punishment.

Those who find fault with the particular form of civil disobedience which I am concerned to justify maintain that breaches of the law, though they may be justified under a despotic regime, can never be justified in a democracy. I cannot see any validity whatever in this contention. There are many ways in which nominally democratic governments can fail to carry out principles which friends of democracy should respect. Take, for example, the case of Ireland before it achieved independence. Formally, the Irish had the same democratic rights as the British. They could send representatives to Westminster and plead their case by all the received democratic processes. But, in spite of this, they were in a minority which, if they had confined themselves to legal methods, would have been permanent. They won their independence by breaking the law. If they had not broken it, they could not have won.

There are many other ways in which governments, which are nominally democratic, fail to be so. A great many questions are so complex that only a few experts can understand them. When the bank rate is raised or lowered, what proportion of the electorate can judge whether it was right to do so? And, if anyone who has no official position criticizes the action of the Bank of England, the only witnesses who can give authoritative evidence will be men responsible for what has been done, or closely connected with those who are responsible. Not only in questions of finance, but still more in military and diplomatic questions, there is in every civilized state a well-developed technique of concealment. If the government wishes some fact to remain unknown, almost all major organs of publicity will assist in concealment. In such cases it often happens that the truth can only be made known, if at all, by persistent and self-sacrificing efforts involving obloquy and perhaps disgrace. Sometimes, if the matter rouses sufficient passion, the truth comes to be known in the end. This happened, for example, in the Dreyfus Case. But where the matter is less sensational the ordinary voter is likely to be left permanently in ignorance.

For such reasons democracy, though much less liable to abuses than dictatorship, is by no means immune to abuses of power by those in authority or by corrupt interests. If valuable liberties are to be preserved there have to be people willing to criticize authority and even, on occasion, to disobey it.

Those who most loudly proclaim their respect for law are in many cases quite unwilling that the domain of law should extend to international relations. In relations between states the only law is still the law of the jungle. What decides a dispute is the question of which side can cause the greatest number of deaths to the other side. Those who do not accept this criterion are apt to be accused of lack of patriotism. This makes it impossible not to suspect that law is only valued where it already exists, and not as an alternative to war.

This brings me at last to the particular form of non-violent civil disobedience which is advocated and practised by the Committee of 100. Those who study nuclear weapons and the probable course of nuclear war are divided into two classes. There are, on the one hand, people employed by governments, and, on the other hand, unofficial people who are actuated by a realization of the dangers and catastrophes which are probable if governmental policies remain unchanged. There are a number of questions in dispute. I will mention a few of them. What is the likelihood of a nuclear war by accident? What is to be feared from fall-out? What proportion of the population is likely to survive an all-out nuclear war? On every one of these questions independent students find that official apologists and policy-makers give answers which, to an unbiased inquirer, appear grossly and murderously misleading. To make known to the general population what independent inquirers believe to be the true answers to those questions is a very difficult matter. Where the truth is difficult to ascertain there is a natural inclination to believe what official authorities assert. This is especially the case when what they assert enables people to dismiss uneasiness as needlessly alarmist. The major organs of publicity feel themselves part of the Establishment and are very reluctant to take a course which the Establishment will frown on. Long and frustrating experience has proved, to those among us who have endeavoured to make unpleasant facts known, that orthodox methods, alone, are insufficient. By means of civil disobedience a certain kind of publicity becomes possible. What we do is reported, though as far as possible our reasons for what we do are not mentioned. The policy of suppressing our reasons, however, has only very partial success. Many people are roused to inquire into questions which they had been willing to ignore. Many people, especially among the young, come to share the opinion that governments, by means of lies and evasions, are luring whole populations to destruction. It seems not unlikely that, in the end, an irresistible popular movement of protest will compel governments to allow their subjects to continue to exist. On the basis of long experience, we are convinced that this object cannot be achieved by law-abiding methods alone. Speaking for myself, I regard this as the most important reason for adopting civil disobedience.

Another reason for endeavouring to spread knowledge about nuclear warfare is the extreme imminence of the peril. Legally legitimate methods of spreading this knowledge have been proved to be very slow, and we believe, on the basis of experience, that only such methods as we have adopted can spread the necessary knowledge before it is too late. As things stand, a nuclear war, probably by accident, may occur at any moment. Each day that passes without such a war is a matter of luck, and it cannot be expected that luck will hold indefinitely. Any day, at any hour, the whole population of Britain may perish. Strategists and negotiators play a leisurely game in which procrastination is one of the received methods. It is urgent that the populations of East and West compel both sides to realize that the time at their disposal is limited and that, while present methods continue, disaster is possible at any moment, and almost certain sooner or later.

There is, however, still another reason for employing non-violent civil disobedience which is very powerful and deserves respect. The programmes of mass extermination, upon which vast sums of public money are being spent, must fill every humane person with feelings of utter horror. The West is told that communism is wicked; the East is told that capitalism is wicked. Both sides deduce that the nations which favour either are to be "obliterated," to use Khrushchev's word. I do not doubt that each side is right in thinking that a nuclear war would destroy the other side's "ism," but each side is hopelessly mistaken if it thinks that a nuclear war could establish its own "ism." Nothing that either East or West desires can result from a nuclear war. If both sides could be made to understand this, it would become possible for both sides to realize that there can be no victory for either, but only total defeat for both. If this entirely obvious fact were publicly admitted in a joint statement by Khrushchev and Kennedy, a compromise method of coexistence could be negotiated giving each side quite obviously a thousand times more of what it wants than could be achieved by war. The utter uselessness of war, in the present age, is completely obvious except to those who have been so schooled in past traditions that they are incapable of thinking in terms of the world that we now have to live in. Those of us who protest against nuclear weapons and nuclear war cannot acquiesce in a world in which each man owes such freedom as remains to him to the capacity of his government to cause many hundreds of millions of deaths by pressing a button. This is to us an abomination, and rather than seem to acquiesce in it we are willing, if necessary, to become outcasts and to suffer whatever obloquy and whatever hardship may be involved in standing aloof from the governmental framework. This thing is a horror. It is something in the shadow of which nothing good can flourish. I am convinced that, on purely political grounds, our reasoned case is unanswerable. But, beyond all political considerations, there is the determination not to be an accomplice in the worst crime that human beings have ever contemplated. We are shocked, and rightly shocked, by Hitler's extermination of six million Jews, but the governments of East and West calmly contemplate the possibility of a massacre at least a hundred times greater than that perpetrated by Hitler. Those who realize the magnitude of this horror cannot even *seem* to acquiesce in the policies from which it springs. It is this feeling, much more than any political calculation, that gives fervour and strength to our movement, a kind of fervour and a kind of strength which, if a nuclear war does not soon end us all, will make our movement grow until it reaches the point where governments can no longer refuse to let mankind survive.

ALEKSANDR SOLZHENITSYN

Live Not By Lies (1974)

The Soviet dissident Aleksandr Solzhenitsyn (1918–2008) was one of his country's greatest writers as well as its loudest critic. Born during the Russian Civil War, Solzhenitsyn was serving as a captain in World War II when he made joking references about the Soviet leader, Josef Stalin, and was arrested and sent to the Gulag, the USSR's prison labor camp system. Having survived eight years there, he was sent into internal exile in Kazakhstan to teach school, but was immediately diagnosed with terminal cancer. The result of this diagnosis was long in coming; he lived another fifty-five years, constantly writing in secret for the first ten years, and then awakening the world with his short novel One Day in the Life of Ivan Denisovich *(1962). After he won the Nobel Prize for Literature in 1970, he became more and more outspoken in his public statements, many of which called for civil disobedience. Meanwhile, he was chronicling the Gulag system, and his arrest by the KGB and deportation to the West set off the publication of "Live Not by Lies" and the documentary history* The Gulag Archipelago.[1] *Solzhenitsyn was one of the few*

---

[1] "You have relations, a family, subordinates and superiors; you are under an influence so powerful that you cannot shake it off; but you can always recognize the truth and refuse to tell a lie about it," declared Leo Tolstoy eighty years before Solzhenitsyn's statement. "You need not declare that you are remaining a landowner, manufacturer, merchant, artist, or writer because it is useful to mankind; that you are governor, prosecutor, or tsar, not because it is agreeable to you, because you are used to it, but for the public good; that you continue to be a soldier, not from fear of punishment, but because you consider the army necessary to society. You can always avoid lying in this way to yourself and to others, and you ought to do so; because the one aim of your life ought to be to purify yourself from falsehood and to confess the truth. And you need only do that and your situation will change directly of itself." *The Kingdom of God is Within You.* Translated by Constance Garnett. Mineola, New York: Dover. Chapter XII, pp. 323–324.

public figures in the world who predicted the political collapse of the USSR. In 1994, he returned to Russia from his place of exile in Vermont.

AT ONE TIME we dared not even to whisper. Now we write and read *samizdat,* and sometimes when we gather in the smoking room at the Science Institute we complain frankly to one another: What kind of tricks are they playing on us, and where are they dragging us? Gratuitous boasting of cosmic achievements while there is poverty and destruction at home. Propping up remote, uncivilized regimes. Fanning up civil war. And we recklessly fostered Mao Tse-tung at our expense—and it will be we who are sent to war against him, and will have to go. Is there any way out? And they put on trial anybody they want, and they put sane people in asylums—always they, and we are powerless.

Things have almost reached rock bottom. A universal spiritual death has already touched us all, and physical death will soon flare up and consume us both and our children—but as before we still smile in a cowardly way and mumble without tongues tied. But what can we do to stop it? We haven't the strength.

We have been so hopelessly dehumanized that for today's modest ration of food we are willing to abandon all our principles, our souls, and all the efforts of our predecessors and all the opportunities for our descendants—but just don't disturb our fragile existence. We lack staunchness, pride and enthusiasm. We don't even fear universal nuclear death, and we don't fear a third world war. We have already taken refuge in the crevices. We just fear acts of civil courage.

We fear only to lag behind the herd and to take a step alone—and suddenly find ourselves without white bread, without heating gas and without a Moscow registration.

We have been indoctrinated in political courses, and in just the same way was fostered the idea to live comfortably, and all will be well for the rest of our lives: You can't escape your environment and social conditions. Everyday life defines consciousness. What does it have to do with us? We can't do anything about it.

But we can—everything. But we lie to ourselves for assurance. And it is not they who are to blame for everything—we ourselves, only we. One can object: But actually you can think anything you like. Gags have been stuffed into our mouths. Nobody wants to listen to us, and nobody asks us. How can we force them to listen? It is impossible to change their minds.

It would be natural to vote them out of office—but there are not elections in our country. In the West people know about strikes and protest demonstrations—but we are too oppressed, and it is a horrible prospect for us: How can one suddenly renounce a job and take to the streets? Yet the other fatal paths probed during the past century by our bitter Russian history are, nevertheless, not for us, and truly we don't need them.

Now that the axes have done their work, when everything which was sown has sprouted anew, we can see that the young and presumptuous people who thought they would make our country just and happy through terror, bloody rebellion and civil war were themselves misled. No thanks, fathers of education! Now we know that infamous methods breed infamous results. Let our hands be clean!

The circle—is it closed? And is there really no way out? And is there only one thing left for us to do, to wait without taking action? Maybe something will happen by itself? It will never happen as long as we daily acknowledge, extol, and strengthen—and do not sever ourselves from—the most perceptible of its aspects: Lies.

When violence intrudes into peaceful life, its face glows with self-confidence, as if it were carrying a banner and shouting: "I am violence. Run away, make way for me—I will crush you." But violence quickly grows old. And it has lost confidence in itself, and in order to maintain a respectable face it summons falsehood as its ally—since violence can conceal itself with nothing except lies, and the lies can be maintained only by violence. And violence lays its ponderous paw not every day and not on every shoulder. It demands from us only obedience to lies and daily participation in lies—all loyalty lies in that.

And the simplest and most accessible key to our self-neglected liberation lies right here: Personal non-participation in lies. Though lies conceal everything, though lies embrace everything, we will be obstinate in this smallest of matters: Let them embrace everything, but not with any help from me.

This opens a breach in the imaginary encirclement caused by our inaction. It is the easiest thing to do for us, but the most devastating for the lies. Because when people renounce lies it simply cuts short their existence. Like an infection, they can exist only in a living organism.

We do not exhort ourselves. We have not sufficiently matured to march into the squares and shout the truth out loud or to express aloud what we think. It's not necessary.

It's dangerous. But let us refuse to say that which we do not think.

This is our path, the easiest and most accessible one, which takes into account our inherent cowardice, already well rooted. And it is much easier—it's dangerous even to say this—than the sort of civil disobedience which Gandhi advocated.

Our path is not to give conscious support to lies about anything whatsoever! And once we realize where lie the perimeters of falsehood each sees them in his own way.

Our path is to walk away from the gangrenous boundary. If we did not paste together the dead bones and scales of ideology, if we did not sew together the rotting rags, we would be astonished how quickly the lies would be rendered helpless and subside.

That which should be naked would then really appear naked before the whole world.

So in our timidity, let each of us make a choice: Whether consciously, to remain a servant of falsehood—of course, it is not out of inclination, but to feed one's family, that one raises his children in the spirit of lies—or to shrug off the lies and become an honest man worthy of respect both by one's children and contemporaries.

And from that day onward he:

Will not henceforth write, sign, or print in any way a single phrase which in his opinion distorts the truth.

Will utter such a phrase neither in private conversation nor in the presence of many people, neither on his own behalf nor at the prompting of someone else, neither in the role of agitator, teacher, educator, nor in a theatrical role.

Will not depict, foster or broadcast a single idea which he can see is false or a distortion of the truth, whether it be in painting, sculpture, photography, technical science or music.

Will not cite out of context, either orally or written, a single quotation so as to please someone, to feather his own nest, to achieve success in his work, if he does not share completely the idea which is quoted, or if it does not accurately reflect the matter at issue.

Will not allow himself to be compelled to attend demonstrations or meetings if they are contrary to his desire or will, will neither take into hand nor raise into the air a poster or slogan which he does not completely accept.

Will not raise his hand to vote for a proposal with which he does not sincerely sympathize, will vote neither openly nor secretly for a person whom he considers unworthy or of doubtful abilities.

Will not allow himself to be dragged to a meeting where there can be expected a forced or distorted discussion of a question.

Will immediately walk out of a meeting, session, lecture, performance or film showing if he hears a speaker tell lies, or purvey ideological nonsense or shameless propaganda.

Will not subscribe to or buy a newspaper or magazine in which information is distorted and primary facts are concealed.

Of course, we have not listed all of the possible and necessary deviations from falsehood. But a person who purifies himself will easily distinguish other instances with his purified outlook.

No, it will not be the same for everybody at first. Some, at first, will lose their jobs. For young people who want to live with truth, this will, in the beginning, complicate their young lives very much, because the required recitations are stuffed with lies, and it is necessary to make a choice.

But there are no loopholes for anybody who wants to be honest: On any given day any one of us will be confronted with at least one of the above-mentioned choices even in the most secure of the technical sciences. Either truth or falsehood: Toward spiritual independence, or toward spiritual servitude.

And he who is not sufficiently courageous even to defend his soul—don't let him be proud of his "progressive" views, and don't let him boast that he is an academician or a people's artist, a merited figure, or a general—let him say to himself: I am in the herd, and a coward. It's all the same to me as long as I'm fed and warm.

Even this path, which is the most modest of all paths of resistance, will not be easy for us. But it is much easier than self-immolation or a hunger strike: The flames will not envelope your body, your eyeballs, will not burst from the heat, and brown bread and clean water will always be available to your family.

A great people of Europe, the Czechoslovaks, whom we betrayed and deceived: Haven't they shown us how a vulnerable breast can stand up even against tanks if there is a worthy heart within it?

You say it will not be easy? But it will be easiest of all possible resources. It will not be an easy choice for a body, but it is only one for a soul. No, it is not an easy path. But there are already people, even dozens of them, who over the years have maintained all these points and live by the truth.

So you will not be the first to take this path, but will join those who have already taken it. This path will be easier and shorter for all of us if we take it by mutual efforts and in close rank. If there are thousands of us, they will not be able to do anything with us. If there are tens of thousands of us, then we would not even recognize our country.

If we are too frightened, then we should stop complaining that someone is suffocating us. We ourselves are doing it. Let us then bow down even more, let us wait, and our brothers the biologists will help to bring nearer the day when they are able to read our thoughts are worthless and hopeless.

And if we get cold feet, even taking this step, then we are worthless and hopeless, and the scorn of Pushkin should be directed to us:

"Why should cattle have the gifts of freedom?

"Their heritage from generation to generation is the belled yoke and the lash."

AUNG SAN SUU KYI

Freedom from Fear (1991)

Born in 1945, the daughter of Burma's hero of independence from Great Britain—General Aung San, who was assassinated in 1947—Aung San Suu Kyi returned to Burma from abroad in 1988. Inspired by Gandhi and committed to democracy and nonviolent protest, she spoke out against the brutal suppression of protesters by U Ne Win's government. After organizing the National League for Democracy party, she was arrested by the military government in 1989. While still under house arrest, she won the Nobel Peace Prize in 1991. For the next two decades Suu Kyi was forbidden communication with the world outside Myanmar (rechristened Burma). After numerous international outcries, she was freed; in 2012, she was elected a member of Myanmar's parliament. In 2015, her party, the NLD, won a major victory in the Myanmar general election, making Aung San Suu Kyi the de facto leader of her country.

"Freedom from Fear" was first released for publication to commemorate the European Parliament's awarding to her of the 1990 Sakharov Prize for Freedom of Thought. The award ceremony took place in her absence at Strasbourg on 10 July 1991.

IT IS NOT power that corrupts but fear. Fear of losing power corrupts those who wield it and fear of the scourge of power corrupts those who are subject to it. Most Burmese are familiar with the four *a-gati*, the four kinds of corruption. *Chanda-gati*, corruption induced by desire, is deviation from the right path in pursuit of bribes or for the sake of those one loves. *Dosa-gati* is taking the wrong path to spite those against whom one bears ill will, and *moha-gati* is aberration due to ignorance. But perhaps the worst of the four is *bhaya-gati*, for not only does *bhaya*, fear, stifle and slowly destroy all sense of right and wrong, it so often lies at the root of the other three kinds of corruption.

Just as *chanda-gati*, when not the result of sheer avarice, can be caused by fear of want or fear of losing the goodwill of those one

162

loves, so fear of being surpassed, humiliated or injured in some way can provide the impetus for ill will. And it would be difficult to dispel ignorance unless there is freedom to pursue the truth unfettered by fear. With so close a relationship between fear and corruption it is little wonder that in any society where fear is rife corruption in all forms becomes deeply entrenched.

Public dissatisfaction with economic hardships has been seen as the chief cause of the movement for democracy in Burma, sparked off by the student demonstrations of 1988. It is true that years of incoherent policies, inept official measures, burgeoning inflation and falling real income had turned the country into an economic shambles. But it was more than the difficulties of eking out a barely acceptable standard of living that had eroded the patience of a traditionally good-natured, quiescent people—it was also the humiliation of a way of life disfigured by corruption and fear. The students were protesting not just against the death of their comrades but against the denial of their right to life by a totalitarian regime which deprived the present of meaningfulness and held out no hope for the future. And because the students' protests articulated the frustrations of the people at large, the demonstrations quickly grew into a nationwide movement. Some of its keenest supporters were businessmen who had developed the skills and the contacts necessary not only to survive but to prosper within the system. But their affluence offered them no genuine sense of security or fulfilment, and they could not but see that if they and their fellow citizens, regardless of economic status, were to achieve a worthwhile existence, an accountable administration was at least a necessary if not a sufficient condition. The people of Burma had wearied of a precarious state of passive apprehension where they were 'as water in the cupped hands' of the powers that be.

> Emerald cool we may be
> As water in cupped hands
> But oh that we might be
> As splinters of glass
> In cupped hands.

Glass splinters, the smallest with its sharp, glinting power to defend itself against hands that try to crush, could be seen as a vivid symbol of the spark of courage that is an essential attribute of those who would free themselves from the grip of oppression. Bogyoke Aung

San regarded himself as a revolutionary and searched tirelessly for answers to the problems that beset Burma during her times of trial. He exhorted the people to develop courage: 'Don't just depend on the courage and intrepidity of others. Each and every one of you must make sacrifices to become a hero possessed of courage and intrepidity. Then only shall we all be able to enjoy true freedom.'

The effort necessary to remain uncorrupted in an environment where fear is an integral part of everyday existence is not immediately apparent to those fortunate enough to live in states governed by the rule of law. Just laws do not merely prevent corruption by meting out impartial punishment to offenders. They also help to create a society in which people can fulfil the basic requirements necessary for the preservation of human dignity without recourse to corrupt practices. Where there are no such laws, the burden of upholding the principles of justice and common decency falls on the ordinary people. It is the cumulative effect of their sustained effort and steady endurance which will change a nation where reason and conscience are warped by fear into one where legal rules exist to promote man's desire for harmony and justice while restraining the less desirable destructive traits in his nature.

In an age when immense technological advances have created lethal weapons which could be, and are, used by the powerful and the unprincipled to dominate the weak and the helpless, there is a compelling need for a closer relationship between politics and ethics at both the national and international levels. The Universal Declaration of Human Rights of the United Nations proclaims that 'every individual and every organ of society' should strive to promote the basic rights and freedoms to which all human beings regardless of race, nationality or religion are entitled. But as long as there are governments whose authority is founded on coercion rather than on the mandate of the people, and interest groups which place short-term profits above long-term peace and prosperity, concerted international action to protect and promote human rights will remain at best a partially realized ideal. There will continue to be arenas of struggle where victims of oppression have to draw on their own inner resources to defend their inalienable rights as members of the human family.

The quintessential revolution is that of the spirit, born of an intellectual conviction of the need for change in those mental attitudes and values which shape the course of a nation's development. A revolution which aims merely at changing official policies and institutions with a view to an improvement in material conditions has little chance of genuine success. Without a revolution of the spirit, the forces which produced the iniquities of the old order would continue to be operative, posing a constant threat to the process of reform and regeneration. It is not enough merely to call for freedom, democracy and human rights. There has to be a united determination to persevere in the struggle, to make sacrifices in the name of enduring truths, to resist the corrupting influences of desire, ill will, ignorance and fear.

Saints, it has been said, are the sinners who go on trying. So free men are the oppressed who go on trying and who in the process make themselves fit to bear the responsibilities and to uphold the disciplines which will maintain a free society. Among the basic freedoms to which men aspire that their lives might be full and uncramped, freedom from fear stands out as both a means and an end. A people who would build a nation in which strong, demo-cratic institutions are firmly established as a guarantee against state-induced power must first learn to liberate their own minds from apathy and fear.

Always one to practise what he preached, Aung San himself constantly demonstrated courage—not just the physical sort but the kind that enabled him to speak the truth, to stand by his word, to accept criticism, to admit his faults, to correct his mistakes, to respect the opposition, to parley with the enemy and to let people be the judge of his worthiness as a leader. It is for such moral cour-age that he will always be loved and respected in Burma—not merely as a warrior hero but as the inspiration and conscience of the nation. The words used by Jawaharlal Nehru to describe Mahatma Gandhi could well be applied to Aung San: 'The essence of his teaching was fearlessness and truth, and action allied to these, always keeping the welfare of the masses in view.'

Gandhi, that great apostle of non-violence, and Aung San, the founder of a national army, were very different personalities, but as there is an inevitable sameness about the challenges of authoritarian rule anywhere at any time, so there is a similarity in the intrinsic qualities of those who rise up to meet the challenge. Nehru, who considered the instillation of courage in the people of India one of Gandhi's greatest achievements, was a political modernist, but as he assessed the needs for a twentieth-century movement for indepen-dence, he found himself looking back to the philosophy of ancient India: 'The greatest gift for an individual or a nation . . . was *abhaya*, fearlessness, not merely bodily courage but absence of fear from the mind.'

Fearlessness may be a gift but perhaps more precious is the courage acquired through endeavour, courage that comes from cultivating the habit of refusing to let fear dictate one's actions, courage that could be described as 'grace under pressure'—grace which is renewed repeatedly in the face of harsh, unremitting pressure.

Within a system which denies the existence of basic human rights, fear tends to be the order of the day. Fear of imprisonment, fear of torture, fear of death, fear of losing friends, family, property or means of livelihood, fear of poverty, fear of isolation, fear of failure. A most insidious form of fear is that which masquerades as common sense or even wisdom, condemning as foolish, reckless, insignificant or futile the small, daily acts of courage which help to preserve man's self-respect and inherent human dignity. It is not easy for a people conditioned by the iron rule of the principle that might is right to free themselves from the enervating miasma of fear. Yet even under the most crushing state machinery courage rises up again and again, for fear is not the natural state of civilized man.

The wellspring of courage and endurance in the face of unbridled power is generally a firm belief in the sanctity of ethical principles combined with a historical sense that despite all setbacks the condition of man is set on an ultimate course for both spiritual and material advancement. It is his capacity for self-improvement and self-redemption which most distinguishes man from the mere brute. At the root of human responsibility is the concept of perfection, the urge to achieve it, the intelligence to find a path towards it, and the will to follow that path if not to the end at least the distance needed to rise above individual limitations and environmental impediments. It is man's vision of a world fit for rational, civilized humanity which leads him to dare and to suffer to build societies free from want and fear. Concepts such as truth, justice and compassion cannot be dismissed as trite when these are often the only bulwarks which stand against ruthless power.

NADEZHDA TOLOKONNIKOVA
(MEMBER OF PUSSY RIOT)

"Words Will Break Cement" (2012)

This essay is Tolokonnikova's closing statement at her trial in Moscow on August 8, 2012. Born in 1989, Tolokonnikova was one of three members of the protest group Pussy Riot who were tried for "hooliganism." That is, they walked into an oligarch-funded cathedral on the Moscow River and played about thirty seconds of a song ("Mother of God, Chase Putin Out"), with the lyrics admonishing the church authorities for supporting President Putin's laws and not Christ's. Tolokonnikova and Maria Alyokhina were sentenced to two years and served sixteen months as "prisoners of conscience" in Russian penal colonies; winners of the Hannah Arendt Prize for Political Thought in 2014, they continue to advocate for human rights. [Essay translated by Masha Gessen for the book Words Will Break Cement, *2012]*

IN THE GREAT scheme of things it's not the three Pussy Riot singers who are on trial here. If it were, what happens here would be of no consequence whatsoever. But it is the entire Russian state system that is on trial here, a system that, to its own detriment, is so enamored of quoting its own cruelty toward the human being, its own indifference toward his honor and integrity—all the bad things that have ever happened in Russian history. The process of imitating

---

* Note by Masha Gessen, translator: Unlike some versions of Pussy Riot's closing statements, these are the speeches as they were spoken during the trial, not as they had been written. I have translated them from transcripts prepared by Elena Kostyuchenko for *Novaya Gazeta*. I have intentionally kept the occasional repetitions, incomplete sentences, and ambiguous or factually incorrect statements (e.g., Putin does not hold international meetings daily or even weekly). These are the statements as Kat, Maria, and Nadya made them, sleep-deprived, drained, and almost entirely deprived of the benefit of one another's intellectual or editorial input.

justice is beginning to resemble closely that of Stalinist *troikas,* I am very sorry to say. We see the same thing here: the investigator, the judge, and the prosecutor make up the court. And on top of it and above it all stands the political demand for repression, which determines the words and actions of all three.

Who is responsible for the action in the Cathedral of Christ the Savior occurring and for the fact that this trial followed the concerts? It is the authoritarian political system. Pussy Riot does opposition art. In other words, it's politics that uses forms created by artists. In any case, it's civic activity that occurs in conditions where basic human rights, civil and political liberties are repressed by a corporate system of state power. Many people who have been having their skin stripped off by the systematic destruction of liberties since the beginning of the 2000s are starting to riot. We were seeking true sincerity and simplicity and we found them in the holy-fool aesthetic of punk performance. Passion, openness, and naiveté exist on a higher ground than do hypocrisy, lying, and false piety used to mask crimes. Top state officials go to church wearing the correct facial expression, but they lie, and in doing so they sin more than we ever did.

We staged our political punk performances because the Russian state system is so rigid, so closed, so caste- based, and its politics so subservient to narrow corporate interests, that it pains us to breathe the very air in this country. We cannot abide this at all, and it forces us to act and live politically. The use of force and coercion to regulate social processes. A situation where key political institutions, the disciplinary structures of the state—the uniformed services, the army, the police, the secret police, and the corresponding means of ensuring political stability: prisons, preventive detentions, the tools of exerting rigid control over citizens' behavior.

We also cannot abide the forced civic passivity of the majority of the population as well as the total domination of the executive branch over the legislative and judicial ones.

In addition, we are sincerely irritated by that which is based on fear and a scandalously low level of political culture, and this level is intentionally maintained by the state system and its helpers. Look at what Patriarch Kirill says: "The Russian Orthodox do not go to demonstrations." We are irritated by the scandalous weakness of horizontal links in society.

We object to the manipulation of public opinion, carried out with ease because the state controls the vast majority of media outlets. Take, for example, the blatant campaign against Pussy Riot, based on the perversion of all facts, undertaken by the mass media with the exception of the very few that manage to maintain independence in this political system, is a good example.

Nonetheless, I am now stating that this situation is authoritarian: this political system is authoritarian. Nonetheless, I am observing a sort of crash of this system where the three Pussy Riot participants are concerned. Because the result for which the system was aiming has not come to pass, unfortunately for the system. Russia has not condemned us. With each day more and more people come to believe in us and to believe us and to think that we should be free and not behind bars. I see that in the people I meet. I meet people who represent the system, who work for it. I see people who are serving time. And with every passing day there are more of them who wish us luck and wish us freedom and say that our political act was justified. People say, "At first we had doubts about whether you should have done what you did." But with every passing day there are more and more people who say to us, "Time has shown that your political act was right. You exposed the sores of this political system. You struck the serpent's nest that has now come back to attack you." These people are trying to do what they can to make our lives easier, and we are very grateful to them for this. We are grateful to the people who are speaking out in support of us on the other side of the fence. There are a huge number of them. I know this. And I know that at this point a huge number of Orthodox believers are speaking out on our behalf, including praying for us, praying for the members of Pussy Riot who are behind bars. We have seen the little book these Orthodox believers are handing out, a little book that contains a prayer for those who are behind bars. This one example is enough to show that there is not one unified group of Orthodox believers as the prosecution is trying to show. It does not exist. And more and more believers are now taking the side of Pussy Riot. They think that what we did should not have brought us five months in pretrial detention and certainly should not bring three years in prison as Mr. Prosecutor would have it.

With every passing day people understand more and more clearly that if the political system turns all its might against three girls who spent a mere thirty seconds performing in the Cathedral of Christ the Savior, that means only that this political system is afraid of the truth, afraid of the sincerity and directness that we bring. We have not lied for a second, we have not lied for one single moment during this trial. Whereas the opposite side lies excessively, and people sense this. People sense the truth. Truth really does have an onto-logical, an existential advantage over lies. The Bible addresses this. In the Old Testament, for example, the way of truth always triumphs over the way of lies. And with every passing day, the way of truth is triumphing more and more, despite the fact that we are behind bars and will probably remain behind bars for a very long time to come.

Madonna had a concert yesterday, and she performed with the words PUSSY RIOT on her back. More and more people are realizing that we are being held here illegally and on the basis of thoroughly falsified charges. I am struck by this. I am struck by the fact that truth really is triumphing over lies even though physically we are here. We have more freedom than the people who are sitting opposite us, on the side of the accusers, because we can say what we want and we do say what we want. Whereas the people over there [Nadya pointed at the prosecutor], they say only that which political censorship allows them to say. They cannot say the words "'Mother of God, chase Putin out,' a punk prayer," they cannot utter those lines in the punk prayer that have to do with the political system. Maybe they think that it would be good to send us to jail because we have spoken out against Putin and his system.

But they cannot say that because they are forbidden. Their mouths are sewn shut, and here they are nothing but puppets, unfortunately. I hope that they realize this and that ultimately they too will choose the way of truth, the way of sincerity and freedom, because it exists on higher ground than rigidity and false piety and hypocrisy.

Rigidity is always the opposite of the search for truth. And in this case, at this trial, we see people who are trying to find some sort of truth on one side and, on the other side, people who want to shackle those who seek the truth. To be human is to err; humans are imperfect. Humans are always striving for wisdom, but it is always elusive. This is exactly how philosophy came to be. This is exactly why a philosopher is a person who loves wisdom and strives for it, but can never possess it. This is exactly what makes him think and act as he does. And this is exactly what moved us to enter the Cathedral of Christ the Savior. And I think that Christianity, as I have understood it studying the Old Testament but especially the New Testament, it supports the search for truth and the constant overcoming of one's self, of what you once were. There is a reason Christ was with the fallen women. He said, 'Help must go to those who have made mistakes, and I forgive them.' But I see none of this in our trial, which purports to represent Christianity. I think it's the prosecution that is affronting Christianity!

The victims' lawyers are starting to disown them. That's how I see it. Two days ago attorney Taratukhin gave a speech in this courtroom in which he said that people should understand that the lawyer does not by any means feel solidarity with people he represents. Apparently the attorney feels ethical unease at representing people who want to see three Pussy Riot participants go to jail. I don't know why they want to see us go to jail, but that's their right. I am just pointing out the fact that the attorney seems to feel shame. Hearing people shout "Shame!" and "Executioners!" at him has touched him after all. An attorney always has to stand for truth and goodness triumphing over evil and lies. It also seems to me that a higher power may be directing the speeches of our opponents: the lawyers keep misspeaking or making mistakes. They keep calling us "victims." They've all done this, including attorney Pavlova, who has a very negative view of us. And yet a higher power of some sort is forcing her to say "victims" about us, not about those whom she is representing. About us.

But I wouldn't affix any labels here. I don't think anyone here is winning or losing; there are no victims and no accused. We need to find a point of contact finally, start a dialogue and commence a joint search for the truth. Strive for wisdom together, be philosophers together rather than simply stigmatize and label people. This is the last thing a person should do, and Christ condemned it.

Here and now, in this court, we are being desecrated. Who would have thought that man and the state system he controls could commit utter, unmotivated evil over and over again. Who would have supposed that history, including the recent frightening experience of the Stalinist Great Terror, has taught us nothing. I want to cry looking at the way the methods of medieval inquisition take center stage in the law-enforcement and court systems of the Russian Federation, of my country. But ever since we were arrested we have lost our ability to cry. Back when we could stage our punk performances, we screamed as loud as we could and knew how to, about the lawlessness of the regime. But they have stolen our voices.

Throughout this trial, they have refused to hear us. I mean, hear. To hear is to listen and think, to strive for wisdom, to be a philosopher. I think every person should, in his heart, strive for this—not just the people who happened to major in some kind of philosophy That means nothing. Formal education by itself means nothing, though attorney Pavlova keeps trying to accuse us of being insufficiently educated. I think that striving is the most important thing, striving to know and to understand. This is something a person can achieve on his own, without the help of an educational institution. No degree, no matter how advanced, can ensure this quality. A human being can possess a lot of knowledge but fail to be human. Pythagorus said that extensive knowledge does not breed wisdom.

I regret that we have to state this here. We serve merely as decorations, as inanimate objects, as bodies delivered to the court-room. If our motions are even considered—and then only follow-ing days of requests, arguments, and struggle—they are invariably denied. But, unfortunately, regrettably for us and for this country, the court listens to the prosecutor, who misrepresents our words and statements over and over again with impunity, rendering them meaningless. The basic principle of equal justice is violated openly—indeed, this seems to be the point.

On July 30, on the first day of the trial, we presented our reac-tion to the charges. Our words were read aloud by attorney Volkova because the court would not then let us speak. This was our first opportunity to speak after five months in captivity. We had been in captivity, we had been behind bars, unable to do anything: we could not make statements, we could not make films, we did not have access to the Internet, and we could not even deliver a piece of paper to one of our lawyers because this is not allowed. On July 30, we spoke out for the first time. We called for contact and dialogue rather than confrontation. We extended a hand to those who have chosen to see us as the enemy. We were laughed at, and the hand we extended was spat upon. We were sincere in what we said, as we always are. We may be childishly naïve in insisting on our truth, but we nonetheless regret none of what we said, includ-ing what we said that day. And even as we are spoken ill of, we will not speak ill in return. Our circumstances are desperate, but we do not despair. We are persecuted, but we have not been abandoned.

---

* Note by Masha Gessen, translator: A prominent television journalist who made three consecutive films about Pussy Riot aimed to show them as heretics and enemies of the Russian state. The films aired on state television in prime time.

Those who are open are easy to humiliate and destroy, but "when I am weak then I am strong."

Listen to us. Listen to us and not to Arkady Mamontov* when he speaks about us. Do not distort every word we say, and let us seek a dialogue, a point of contact with the country, which is our country too and not just Putin's and the patriarch's. Like Solzhenitsyn, I believe that in the end, words will break cement. Solzhenitsyn wrote, "So the word is more sincere than concrete? So the word is not a trifle? Then may noble people begin to grow, and their word will break cement."

Kat, Maria, and I are in jail. We are in a cage. But I don't think that we have been defeated. Just as the dissidents were not defeated. They were lost in psychiatric wards and the jails, but it was they who pronounced the regime's verdict. The art of creating the image of an era knows not winners and losers. The same way as the OBERIU** poets remained artists, truly inexplicable and incomprehensible, even after being purged in 1937. [The poet] Alexander Vvedensky wrote, "The inexplicable pleases us, and the incomprehensible is our friend." According to his official death certificate, Vvedensky died December 20, 1941. Cause of death is not known. He may have caught dysentery in the prison transport, or he may have caught a bullet from one of the guards. It happened somewhere along the railroad line from Voronezh to Kazan. Pussy Riot are Vvedensky's students and disciples. We consider his principle of the bad rhyme to be our own. He wrote, "It happens that two possible rhymes come to mind, a good one and a bad one. I choose the bad one. It is sure to be the right one."

"The incomprehensible is our friend." The OBERIUs' elevated and refined pursuits, their search for thought at the edge of meaning, ultimately cost them their lives, taken by the senseless and truly inexplicable Great Terror. They paid with their lives to show that they had been right to believe that senselessness and lack of logic expressed their era best. They made art into history. The price of taking part in making history is always disproportionately large for

---

* Note by Masha Gessen, translator: A prominent television journalist who made three consecutive films about Pussy Riot aimed to show them as heretics and enemies of the Russian state. The films aired on state television in prime time.
** Note by Masha Gessen, translator: The Union of Real Art, a collective of futurist artists, writers, and musicians in the 1920s and '30s.

the individual and his life. But it is also the meaning of human existence. "To be poor but enrich many. To have nothing but possess everything." The OBERIU dissidents are considered dead, but they are living. They have been punished but not killed.

Do you happen to remember why the young Dostoyevsky was sentenced to death? He was guilty only of having immersed himself in socialist theory. A group of freethinkers who gathered at Petrashevsky's apartment on Fridays discussed the work of George Sand. Toward the end of these Friday gatherings Dostoyevsky recited [literary critic Vissarion] Belinsky's letter to Gogol, filled, according to the court's conclusion, with—and here I want you to pay attention—"impudent statements against the Orthodox Church and the executive power." Dostoyevsky prepared to die. He spent, as he later wrote, ten "terrible, endlessly frightening" minutes waiting to be executed. Then his sentence was commuted to four years of hard labor followed by military service.

Socrates was accused of exerting a bad influence on young people with his philosophical discussions and of failing to recognize the gods of Athens. Socrates had a strong sense of an inner divine voice and he was by no means an enemy of the gods, as he stated repeatedly. But what did it matter, when Socrates annoyed the influential citizens of Athens with his critical, dialectical, and unbiased thinking? Socrates was sentenced to death. He declined his students' offers to help him escape and coolly drank the horn of poison, of hemlock, and died.

And have you perhaps forgotten how Stephen, the disciple of the apostles, ended his earthly life? "Then they secretly induced men to say, 'We have heard him speak blasphemous words against Moses and against God.' And they stirred up the people, the elders and the scribes, and they came up to him and dragged him away and brought him before the Council. They put forward false witnesses who said, 'This man incessantly speaks against this holy place and the Law.'" He was found guilty and stoned to death.

I also hope that you all remember well how the Jews answered Christ: "It is not for good works that we are going to stone you but for blasphemy." And finally we would do well to keep in mind the following characterization of Christ: "He is demon-possessed and raving mad."

I think that if the czars, the elders, the presidents, the premiers, the people, and the judges of this world knew well and understood the meaning of the phrase "I desire mercy, not sacrifice," they would not judge the innocent. But our rulers are in a rush to judge, never to show mercy. We should, incidentally, thank Dmitry Anatolyevich Medvedev for another in a series of remarkable aphorisms. He defined his term as president with the slogan "Freedom is better than unfreedom." Now Putin's third term may come to be characterized by a new aphorism: "Jail is better than stoning."

I ask you to think carefully about the following idea. Montaigne expressed it in his *Essays* in the sixteenth century. He wrote, "It is putting a very high value on one's conjectures, to have a man roasted alive because of them." And should flesh-and-blood people be tried and sent to jail based merely on the prosecution's suppositions, ones that have no basis in fact? We never have nor do we now have feelings of hatred or enmity on the basis of religion. As a result, our accusers have had to find people willing to bear false witness. One of them, Matilda Ivashchenko, felt ashamed and did not show up for court. That left the false testimony of Messrs. Troitsky and Ponkin as well as Ms. Abramenkova. There is no other evidence of enmity or hatred. If the court were honest and truthful, it would have to rule inadmissible the opinion of so-called experts, simply because it is not an objective scholarly text but a filthy, fraudulent scrap of paper that harkens back to the Middle Ages and the Inquisition. There is no other evidence that in any way points to motive.

The prosecution shies away from citing Pussy Riot song lyrics, because they would present the most obvious evidence of the lack of motive. I am going to quote something I like very much. I think this is very important. This is an interview we gave to the newsweekly *Russkiy Reporter* after the performance at the Cathedral of Christ: "We have respect for religion, including the Orthodox religion. This is precisely why we are outraged that the great, kind Christian philosophy has been used in such a filthy manner. We are raging because we see the best and finest that exists today being violated." We are still raging. And we feel real pain looking at all of this.

Every single defense witness has testified to the lack of any expression of hatred or enmity on our parts, even when they were asked to speak only to our individual personalities. In addition, I ask you to consider the results of the psychological and psychiatric evaluation conducted at the investigator's request in pretrial detention. The expert testified that the central values of my life are "justice, mutual respect, humanity, equality, and liberty." This was his expert opinion.

This was a man who does not know me personally. And I suspect that Detective Ranchenkov would have wanted the expert to write something different. But it seems that people who love and value the truth are in the majority after all. Just as the Bible says.

And in conclusion I would like to quote a Pussy Riot song. Strange as it may seem, all of their songs turned out to be prophetic. Among other things, we prophesied that "the head of the KGB and the chief saint march the protesters to pretrial detention under guard." But what I want to quote now is, "Open the doors, rip off your epaulettes, taste the smell of freedom with us!" That's all.